# The Ultimate Plague

# The Ultimate Plague

And how to avoid it!

Philip J. Gentlesk

LIBERTY HILL PRESS

Liberty Hill Publishing
2301 Lucien Way #415
Maitland, FL 32751
407.339.4217
www.libertyhillpublishing.com

© 2022 by Philip J. Gentlesk

All rights reserved solely by the author. The author guarantees all contents are original and do not infringe upon the legal rights of any other person or work. No part of this book may be reproduced in any form without the permission of the author.

Due to the changing nature of the Internet, if there are any web addresses, links, or URLs included in this manuscript, these may have been altered and may no longer be accessible. The views and opinions shared in this book belong solely to the author and do not necessarily reflect those of the publisher. The publisher therefore disclaims responsibility for the views or opinions expressed within the work.

Unless otherwise noted, all scripture quotes are taken from the HOLY BIBLE, New International Version. Copyright 1973, 1978, and 1984 by International Bible Society. Used by permission of Zondervan Bible Publishing House. All rights reserved.

Scripture quotations marked (NASB) are taken from the New American Standard Bible (NASB) Copyright ©1960, 1962, 1963, 1968, 1971, 1972, 1973, 1975, 1977, 1995 by The Lockman Foundation, La Habra, CA. All rights reserved. Used by Permission. www.lockman.org.

Scripture quotations marked (NKJV) are taken from the New King James Version®. Copyright © 1982 by Thomas Nelson. Used by permission. All rights reserved.

Scripture quotations marked (NLT) are taken from the Holy Bible, New Living Translation, copyright ©1996, 2004, 2015 by Tyndale House Foundation. Used by permission of Tyndale House Publishers, Carol Stream, Illinois 60188. All rights reserved.

Scripture quotations marked (TLB) are taken from The Living Bible copyright © 1971. Used by permission of Tyndale House Publishers, Carol Stream, Illinois 60188. All rights reserved.ww

Paperback ISBN-13: 978-1-6628-4289-4
Hard Cover ISBN-13: 978-1-6628-4290-0
Ebook ISBN-13: 978-1-6628-4291-7

# DEDICATION

This book is dedicated to my sister Maryjane Kennedy, a nurse for over 50 years, and her husband Ed. Both are very giving of their time, talent and treasure. Maryjane is the solid rock of the family, always intense about her tennis and golf, but extremely giving of her time to all that need her skills. Ed would give you the shirt off his back if you asked for it. They have two great children who exhibit the same love for their fellow man.

# TABLE OF CONTENTS

CHAPTER ONE ~ A Deadly Enemy in a
World Unprepared. . . . . . . . . . . . . . . . . . . . . . . . . 1

CHAPTER TWO ~ Our Time is Growing Short . . . . . . . . 9

CHAPTER THREE ~ The Miracle of Israel . . . . . . . . . . 15

CHAPTER FOUR ~ The "Foolishness" of
God's Mercy. . . . . . . . . . . . . . . . . . . . . . . . . . . . 23

CHAPTER FIVE ~ The Struggle Continues:
The Story of Jacob & Esau. . . . . . . . . . . . . . . . . 29

CHAPTER SIX ~ Israel: The Center of the World? . . . . 35

CHAPTER SEVEN ~ What Does All This Have
To Do With You? . . . . . . . . . . . . . . . . . . . . . . . 47

CHAPTER EIGHT ~ Life, Death, and
Everything In Between . . . . . . . . . . . . . . . . . . . 57

CHAPTER NINE ~ Discovering the Joy of Obedience. . 69

CHAPTER TEN ~ Fill the Earth . . . . . . . . . . . . . . . . . . 75

# CHAPTER ONE

# A DEADLY ENEMY IN A WORLD UNPREPARED

*"Do not be afraid of those who kill the body but cannot kill the soul. Rather, be afraid of the One who can destroy both soul and body in hell." (Matthew 10:28)*

Over the past year and a half, the world has been battling a deadly illness we all know as COVID-19. This tiny little virus, too small to be seen with the naked eye, has killed, according to the most recent statistics I've seen, 600,000 Americans and three million people worldwide.

This is terrible, of course, and people remain divided over how best to combat this insidious disease. Do masks really help? Are the various vaccines really safe? Does social distancing do any good? And some question whether the virus is as dangerous and deadly as some say it is.

But my point in all of this is that when the virus first arrived on the scene, and it became apparent that it had the capacity to kill, all the forces of science, medicine, industry, and government were marshalled against it. No expense was spared, no stone left unturned, in the search for a cure.

Those in authority realized that something drastic had to be done to save lives, and it was only a matter of months before several different vaccines were available.

COVID-19 is only the latest in a long line of attacks on humanity. Attacks that I believe have been launched by our ancient enemy—Satan.

## MORE DANGEROUS THAN COVID-19

The truth is that we have been plagued by another terminal sickness ever since the first days of history. It causes far more death and destruction than COVID-19 ever could, and yet most people go blithely about their business as if it doesn't exist at all.

This sickness is sin. The mere mention of the word causes the darkened mind to rebel in denial. We hear this word used less and less these days.

Most people (and dictionaries) define sin first as an offense or immoral act against moral or religious law. With the turning away of our country, and even the world, from the acknowledgment of God and who He is, many refuse to admit the existence of a moral law. Rather than defining an action as sin or sinful, society prefers to use softer words, such as *issue*, *weakness*, *problem*, *shortcoming*, or *struggle*.

Sin, in the form of corruption, runs rampant in our streets today and has invaded our Senate, House of Representatives, and even the Executive Branch. This corruption has many faces: bribery, graft, embezzlement, cronyism, nepotism, and lobbying, to name a few.

We've seen corruption waste taxpayers' money and negate important community projects with the use of inferior building materials. As a result, sin has eroded the trust we once had in public and political sectors. We have become skeptical of everything a politician says and suspect the facts to be "spun" according to a specific agenda.

We have become a "dog-eat-dog" society. People are self-centered, narcissistic, judgmental, foul-mouthed, promiscuous, and angry. We are a country that needs change, or we will be in danger of starting a civil war the likes of which this world has not experienced.

Proverbs 20:24 tells us, *"A person's steps are directed by the Lord. How then can anyone understand their own way?"* As human beings, we are subject to God. Men and women may make their plans, but God guides their steps. In His wisdom, He is constantly moving us to choices that are in our best interests. When we, as Christians, wander to a path that will eventually produce nothing good, His nudges will reshape our walk and guide us back to His will.

This proverb teaches us humility regarding our choices in life. We should never think we are in total control.

Similarly, *"A man's heart plans his way, but the Lord directs his steps"* (Proverbs 16:9 NKJV). For man to plan his way is good when we consider that we are made in the image of God, but, again, we must always remember that it is the Lord who directs our steps. Having the ability to make plans for ourselves should not lead us to thinking we are lords of our lives. All our plans should be held in humility before God, and we must always surrender to His will.

James 4:15 reminds us that, when we make our plans, we ought to say, *"If the Lord wills, we shall live and do this or that."*

Your beginning—your birth—in Camden, New Jersey, or Milton, Delaware, or anywhere in the world--has been approved by God. You have an approval stamp from your Creator.

You do have choices, but God sees those choices before you even think them. God has all of time within His view. He exists outside of time and space. He sees the beginning of our lives in our mothers' wombs, and He sees us in our caskets.

The Bible tells us in 1 Timothy 2:4 that God *"desires all men to be saved and to come to the knowledge of the truth"* (NKJV).

Regarding sin—in our lives, our relationships, our country—we must all understand that God alone renders the ultimate verdict. A final door awaits us all. That door is death. All the lies and mistrust have far-reaching effects. We all, including politicians and those who have authority and power of any kind, will be required to answer for all we have said and done.

*"All the nations will be gathered before Him, and He will separate the people one from another, as a shepherd separates the sheep from the goats"* (Matthew 25:32).

Where do you see yourself? Bound for Heaven or bound for Hell? How do you live your life? By what manual or set of rules or standards do you live? There are the rules of "dos and don'ts," and there is living under grace.

All religions have rules. In order to be a "member," you must adhere to sets of regulations that are imposed by the hierarchy of that particular belief system. Catholics have over 1,700 canon laws. The Jewish tradition (Torah) includes 613 commandments. The Muslim faith has five different schools of Sharia law. There are four Sunni doctrines and one Shia doctrine. For any man to adhere to all of these rules is next to impossible.

What do we do? Let's go back to the beginning.

God created humankind to live forever. God also made man to depend on Him. In fact, the entire universe depends on God. He keeps the earth and the moon in their orbits. He orchestrates the rising and setting of the sun. He produces food and water to feed us. Everything is in and by His hand.

So where did it all go wrong? When did we stop depending on God and begin depending on ourselves?

## WILL MORTAL MAN DARE TO CHALLENGE GOD?

Truth be told, we, as humans, have no right to question God about anything. We must understand that He alone knows what is best for us and trust Him to bring that about. Yet, many people refuse to put their trust in God, because they don't understand how a good God can allow evil to exist.

In the beginning, God examined the world He created and said it was good (Genesis 1:31). God did not create the devil in his present form. Lucifer was created at the highest level of the celestial hierarchy. He was in the first sphere of angels, or the Seraphim, Cherubim, Thrones. His name means "Morning Star."

He was anointed as a "Guardian Cherub" and was on the holy mount of God, walking among the fiery stones. He was created blameless until weakness was found in him. In Ezekiel 28:17, we learn of his beauty and that he corrupted his wisdom because of his splendor. In other words, he sinned.

How did Lucifer sin? He was beautiful beyond words, and he allowed his pride to rear its ugly head. He wanted to be worshipped. He thought himself to be equal with God.

Lucifer was told (Isaiah 14:12-15) that he would be brought down to Sheol *"to the lowest depths of the pit."* He became Satan (which means "adversary") and fell from heaven, taking a third of the angels with him. These fallen angels became demons and do the bidding of Satan. The work of this demonic network, according to John 10:10, is to *"steal, kill, and destroy."*

The bottom line is that we were all born with hell as our final destination because we are descended from Adam. We might think that we would not have sinned if we had been Adam. But Adam and Eve were light years ahead of us in intelligence. Humankind lost about 90 percent of our mental capacity when Adam sinned, as today we only use approximately 10 percent of our brains.

But God never stopped loving man. In His great love, He provided a way for us to be reconciled and reunited with our Creator. We were powerless to reconcile ourselves to God because sin stood in the way. We could do nothing. But God gave us His Son Jesus Christ to save us. Jesus took the punishment for our sin upon His own body. He was beaten almost to death, and then nailed to a rough wooden cross—slowly dying while He hung suspended for hours, a humiliating spectacle for those who mocked Him and laughed at Him. He didn't have to do that. But He chose to do it for you and me. His blood is the one and only "vaccine" that will cure us from sin—the worst and most deadly pandemic that ever existed. A Coronavirus may destroy the body, but sin destroys the soul for all eternity!

All we need do is put our trust in Jesus and acknowledge that we are sinners and need Him. We must accept His grace. (You may have heard GRACE described as "**G**od's **r**edemption [or righteousness or riches] **at C**hrist's expense.")

*"Trust in the Lord with all your heart and do not lean on your own understanding"* (Proverbs 3:5).

Not leaning on our own understanding means that, rather than having self-assurance and relying on ourselves, we have confidence that God always does what is best. If we put God first, everything else will be cared for.

> *"For the time will come when they will not endure sound doctrine; but after their own lusts shall they heap to themselves teachers, having itching ears; and they shall turn away their ears from the truth, and shall be turned unto fables"* (2 Timothy 4:3).

There will always be pseudo teachers who say what we want to hear, and we eagerly follow false trails that only lead to our destruction. This was true in the early Church, and it's true today.

Every culture has developed its own man-based wisdom in answer to questions about God and what He does, has done, or will do. No man has ever seen God, but we have all seen His footprints in the sands of life. In time, He will lead to Heaven all those who accept His plan for salvation through Jesus Christ. Those who reject the sacrifice made in the blood of Jesus to follow lies devised by the devil will find themselves in Hell. This includes the great lie that there are other ways to Heaven apart from Jesus.

# CHAPTER TWO

# OUR TIME IS GROWING SHORT

> "But mark this: There will be terrible times in the last days. People will be lovers of themselves, lovers of money, boastful, proud, abusive, disobedient to their parents, ungrateful, unholy, without love, unforgiving, slanderous, without self-control, brutal, not lovers of the good, treacherous, rash, conceited, lovers of pleasure rather than lovers of God—having a form of godliness but denying its power. Have nothing to do with such people." (2 Timothy 3:1-5)

The Bible tells us that the earth we live on will not last forever. There will come a time when God will destroy this planet and everything on it. Even so, those who belong to Him have nothing at all to fear, because they will be evacuated before that terrible day of destruction comes. After that, we will live forever on a new Earth that is perfect in every way. It will be the paradise that our present home was meant to be—before sin entered the picture and corrupted everything.

In recent days, we have witnessed many events that portend the advent of end times. These include:

- **The creation** of nuclear weapons capable of the extermination of humankind
- **The rebirth** of Israel as a nation
- **The re-emergence** of the old Roman Empire
- **The Middle East** as a focal point for economics, politics, and wars
- **The divorce rate** soaring to above percent
- **Crime rates** up over 500 percent
- **Homosexuality** and transgender behavior accepted as a proper lifestyle
- **Terrorism** of all sorts
- **Abortion,** drugs, materialism, humanism, famine, earthquakes, etc.
- **The increase** of demonic activity
- **The ability** to broadcast to the entire world through computers and cell phones

Man's belief systems determine his future. God created man with a spiritual capacity, and our minds continually look for something to give us answers to our deepest questions.

The first victims of spiritual famine are the young. Today they are being supplied with a non-existence of truth. Do any of us really believe the news reports? We are fed lies and more lies. Second Thessalonians 2:11 gives us a sobering reminder of what God can do when He knows someone will not change his mind. *"...and for this reason God will send upon them a deluding influence so that they might believe what is false."*

Our families are being filled with the false philosophy of materialism. We admire celebrities and professional athletes who own mansions in multiple locations and drive expensive, exotic cars. The generation we live in has no use for God and has made idols of possessions and position.

Amos 8:14 describes those who have given in to this idolatry. They will fall and never rise again. Do not be one of these!

I assure you that I am not jealous of and do not begrudge those who have made millions. My desire is to see them in Heaven. Sadly, those who attain great riches often believe they have no need for God. Sin has an easy entrance into their lives. And the more sinful a generation becomes, the less truth the people will tolerate. Take another look at the Scripture I put at the beginning of this chapter (2 Timothy 3:1-4).

God owes us nothing but has given us everything. He blesses those who follow in His way.

## GOD IS ALWAYS TRUTHFUL

We can have confidence in the Word of God. Numbers 23:19 tells us that *"God is not a man, that He should lie."* In Hebrews 6:8, we're also told it is impossible for God to lie. *"So that by two unchangeable things in which it is impossible for God to lie, we who have taken refuge would have strong encouragement to hold firmly to the hope set before us."*

The New Living Translation puts it this way: *"So God has given both His promise and His oath."*

What does all this mean? Literally, it means two things are unchangeable and absolutely reliable. The first "thing" speaks to the nature of God. He is all powerful (see Psalm 68:34, Job 42:2); He cannot change (Malachi 3:6, James 1:17), and He cannot lie, (Numbers 23:19). Because of these attributes—because of God's innate nature—all His promises are true; they are all a certainty.

Secondly, His Word, the Holy Bible, is truth. What God promised in world events (history), He has done. Consider what is happening globally today.

If you look at most world maps, you'll notice the country near the very center is Israel, and the center of Israel is Jerusalem. Why is this important? God does nothing by chance. First, read John 1:3,

*"All things were made by Him: and without Him was not anything made that was made."*

Now look at Ecclesiastes 7:14 (NASB),

*"On the day of prosperity be happy, but on the day of adversity consider: God has made the one as well as the other so that a person will not discover anything that will come after him."*

It is apparent that God took a lowly bunch of nomads who lived in a desert (Sinai, which means "thorn"), then placed them in a land that would become the very center of this earth. Though they were poor and ignorant, God told them they would become His people. *"You only have I chosen among all the families of the earth"* (Amos 3:2). And then God added, *"I will punish you for all your wrongdoing."*

They were called, sovereignly chosen by God, to be a kingdom of priests and a holy nation. They were to be a covenant people, a bright light to the world. They were sinners like the rest of mankind. A poor ragtag group of desert wanderers, yet God chose them.

You will find throughout the Bible that God uses ordinary men and women to accomplish mighty things. (Later in this book, we will talk about those who are "lowly" in the estimation of the world.)

God did not create us so that we could live for our own pleasures. Satan knew what to do after the fall of Adam and

Eve. While the devil is unable to create anything, he set about perverting the good things God created.

One of these good things is sex. God commanded Adam and Eve to go forth and multiply. And He made the process enjoyable for both men and women and instituted that the act was only to take place within the bounds of matrimony.

Satan twisted what was meant to be a holy union into fornication, promiscuity, adultery, prostitution, sex trafficking, bestiality, feminism, and homosexuality. None of these things are God's will.

Food. Sports. Movies. The list of "pleasures" is almost endless. These are acceptable in and of themselves. However, the devil has found ways to pollute them all. Procreation became twisted, and man went for it. A good appetite often leads to gluttony. Sports are harmless in themselves, but many have made sports—and athletes—into idols.

Anything that takes the place of God in our lives is an idol, an abomination.

We are all guilty. Many only provide for their loved ones after their own needs have been met. They prefer to play golf or shop on Sunday mornings instead of going to church.

On May 8, 2021, Megan Rohrer was elected to serve a six-year term as bishop of the Sierra Pacific Synod of the Evangelical Lutheran Church in America. She prefers to be referred to as they/them/their instead of she/her/hers. In other words, she refuses to see herself as one gender or another. It's true. The (ELCA) Evangelical Lutheran Church in America has appointed the denomination's first transgender bishop.[1] What would the prophets think of this? I believe it is another sure sign of the Lord's imminent return.

---

[1] https://www.livinglutheran.org/2021/05/megan-rohrer-elected-bishop-of-elca-sierra-pacific-synod/

A friend told me about attending a Christmas concert at a church last year. Before the concert began an announcement was made that "There are two restrooms in the foyer. On the left, you'll find a restroom for those who define themselves as female, and on the right, you'll find one for those who self-define as male." What is the world coming to? The Bible tells us that in the beginning,

*"God created mankind in his own image, in the image of God he created them; male and female he created them"* (Genesis 1:27).

People are shaking their fists at God and demanding to know, "Why did you make me like this?"
Listen to this word of warning:

*"In the past God overlooked such ignorance, but now he commands all people everywhere to repent. For he has set a day when he will judge the world with justice by the man he has appointed. He has given proof of this to everyone by raising him from the dead"* (Acts 17:30-31).

## CHAPTER THREE

# THE MIRACLE OF ISRAEL

*"The LORD said to Abram ...'Look around from where you are, to the north and south, to the east and west. All the land that you see I will give to you and your offspring forever. I will make your offspring like the dust of the earth, so that if anyone could count the dust, then your offspring could be counted. Go, walk through the length and breadth of the land, for I am giving it to you.'"*
*(Genesis 13:14-17)*

Despite man's disobedience, God is faithful and will keep His promises. For example, He promised Israel—not the Church—a land. Israel today is not the entirety of the land God originally gave them.

"On today's map, the land God has stated belongs to Israel includes everything modern-day Israel possesses, plus all of the territory occupied by the Palestinians (the West Bank and Gaza), plus some of Egypt and Syria, plus all of Jordan, plus some of Saudi Arabia and Iraq. Thus, Israel currently possesses only a fraction of the land God has promised;

the rest of their inheritance likely awaits the return of the Messiah, Jesus Christ."[2]

A review of a few prophecies that allude to this fact will help you determine what you believe. In Ezekiel 39, we learn of the final battle and God's defeat of the nations that have come against Israel. In verse 7, He says, *"So I will make My holy name known in the midst of My people Israel, and I will not let them profane My holy name anymore. Then the nations shall know that I am the Lord, the Holy One in Israel."*

Bill Salus, of Lamb & Lion Ministries, wrote a great book titled, *"Psalm 83, the Missing Prophecy Revealed: How Israel Becomes the Next Mideast Superpower."* Let's take a look at Psalm 83.

"God, do not remain quiet; Do not be silent and, God, do not be still. For behold, Your enemies make an uproar, and those who hate You have exalted themselves. They make shrewd plans against Your people, and conspire together against Your treasured ones.

> *"They have said, 'Come, and let's wipe them out as a nation, so that the name of Israel will no longer be remembered.' For they have conspired together with one mind; They make a covenant against You: The tents of Edom and the Ishmaelites, Moab and the Hagrites; Gebal, Ammon, and Amalek, Philistia with the inhabitants of Tyre; Assyria also has joined them; they have become a help to the children of Lot"* (Psalm 83:1-8).

Verse 9 continues with the Psalmist saying to deal with them as with Midian. As with Sisera and Jabin city) and Jabin (king of Canaan, the commander of his army was Sisera) at the

---

[2] https://www.gotquestions.org/Israel-land.html

torrent of Rishon, who were destroyed at En-dor (Canaanite City), who became as dung for the ground. And to make their nobles like Oreb and Zeeb (two generals of Midian that Gideon killed in Judges 7:15-25) and their princes like Zebah and Zalmunna (two kings who invaded Israel) and said, *"Let us take for ourselves the pastures of God for a possession"* (Psalm 83:12).

Psalm 83 is a *"Song of Asaph,"* who was a singer and songwriter for David and Solomon. This psalm is a prayer for help when war threatens. Asaph, a prophet, included prophesy in his musical compositions. Here, Asaph asks God to behold Israel's crisis and to regard those enemies as God's own enemies.

The hand of God remains on Israel even today. Through all the persecutions God's Chosen People have endured, including the Holocaust, the Jewish population in the world has continued to increase. The devil has tried time and again to eradicate the Jews, but he always fails. Let's look at just three examples.

In Moses' day, Pharaoh decreed that all male Hebrews were to be killed at birth.

> *"Then Pharaoh gave this order to all his people: 'Every Hebrew boy that is born you must throw into the Nile, but let every girl live'"* (Exodus 1:22).

Nearly 1500 years later, Satan made another attempt to eradicate the Jews. Following the announcement by the kings who were following the star and searching for He who would be born "King of the Jews," Herod decreed that all males two years of age and younger in the vicinity of Bethlehem were to be slaughtered.

While there are varying theories on the number of babies killed, Coptic sources estimated that over 144,000 innocents perished.[3]

Another major attempt to annihilate the Jews was instigated by Adolph Hitler during the Holocaust. The U.S. Holocaust Memorial Museum estimates that 6,273,676 Jewish lives were lost. This amounts to 63% of the Jewish population in twenty countries.[4]

These are just three examples. World history speaks to other attempts in the form of wars against Israel. The biblical book of Esther tells how a young queen saved the Jews from another plot to destroy them.

Why such hatred toward the nation of Israel? Simple. God loves His people and Satan hates them. These are the people God established through Abraham. These are the people through whom God sent His Son and His plan of salvation. It was the Jews who preserved and protected the Old Testament scriptures. Satan's desire is to pervert God's plan and thwart Him at every turn.

## WHY THE CONFLICT BETWEEN ISRAEL AND THE ARAB NATIONS?

So much of the conflict in the world today stems from the Middle Eastern conflict between Jews and Arabs. When did this begin and, more importantly, when will it end?

Genesis 11:31 tells us that Terah took his son, Abram (God later changed his name to Abraham), Abram's wife, Sarai (later changed to Sarah), his grandson (Lot), and together

---

[3] https://melkite.org/faith/sunday-scriptures/infants-harvested-like-wheat

[4] https://www.jewishvirtuallibrary.org/estimated-number-of-jews-killed-in-the-final-solution

they set out from their homeplace, Ur of the Chaldeans in Mesopotamia, to go to Canaan. However, when they came to a place called Harran, they settled there.

After the death of Terah, God spoke to Abram, blessing him and telling him to leave his country, taking his people and his father's household, and go to the land God would show him.

Genesis 12:2-3 reveals the amazing promise God made toward Abraham:

*"I will make you into a great nation, and I will bless you;*

*I will make your name great, and you will be a blessing. I will bless those who bless you, and whoever curses you I will curse; and all peoples on earth will be blessed through you."*

Abram was seventy-five years old when he did as God commanded and set out from Harran. He took his wife Sarai, his nephew Lot, all their possessions, plus the servants and slaves they had acquired in Harran.

Genesis 13:2 tells us that Abram had become a very wealthy man through the accumulation of livestock, plus silver and gold. He lived in the land for many years before gaining possession of it. In Genesis 15, the Lord made a promise to Abram that his descendants would outnumber the stars in the sky and identified Himself as the Lord who had brought him out of Ur to give him possession of the land.

When Abram asked the Lord how he could know for sure that he would gain possession of the land, the Lord made a covenant with him. He told him that his descendants would spend four hundred years in captivity. (This later occurred when Abraham's great-grandson Joseph became an Egyptian slave and then rose to power. Under Joseph's command, the Egyptian people set aside large quantities of foodstuffs, which would later help them survive a long, terrible famine. It was during this famine that the rest of Joseph's family fled from Canaan to Egypt to escape starvation. Eventually, when their numbers grew and the Egyptians felt threatened by them, Abraham's descendants were taken into captivity).

But the Lord also renewed His promise to Abram regarding the land, saying:

> *"To your descendants I have given this land; from the river of Egypt as far as the great river, the river Euphrates: the Kenite and the Kenizzite and the Kadmonite and the Hittite and the Perizzite and the Rephaim and the Amorite and the Canaanite and the Girgashite and the Jebusite"* (Genesis 15:18).

A little background on who the people were who currently inhabited the land:

- The Kenites were coppersmiths and metal workers living in the Levant.
- The Kenizzites most likely inhabited some part of modern-day Syria.
- The Kadmonites were a tribe of Canaanites who inhabited the promised land east of the Jordan.
- The Hittites were an important Anatolian tribe who inhabited the land known today as Turkey, Syria, Lebanon, and Cyprus.
- The Perizzites were farmers and peasants of the day (what we might call urban people) who lived in al-Sa'l (Basrah).
- The Kadmonites were the only oriental tribe in Canaan.
- The Hittites were a mighty nation living in what is today Syria.

- The Rephaim were a very tall people, probably located near the future Jerusalem.
- The Amorites were a Semitic people from the Levant (Syria).
- The Canaanites were an indigenous people, encompassing much of today's Lebanon, Israel, and Jordan.
- The Girgashites were also indigenous to the land of Canaan (modern Syria, Lebanon, Jordan, etc.).
- The Jebusites are identified as a Canaanite tribe living in the small area around what later became Jerusalem.

Today, descendants of these people continue to surround Israel and constantly test the Jewish people's resolve and patience.

**The Psalm 83 Confederates:**

- Edom (present-day Palestinians)
- Ishmael (Saudis)
- Moab (Palestinians and Jordanians)
- Hagarenes (present-day Egyptians)
- Gebal (Hezbollah and northern Lebanese)
- Ammon (Palestinians)
- Amalek (Arabs of the Sinai area)
- Philistia (represents Hamas of the Gaza Strip)
- Tyre (represents Hezbollah and the southern Lebanese)
- Assyria (equates to Syrians and northern Iraq)

## MODERN ENEMIES OF ISRAEL

*Hezbollah* is a bitter enemy of the Israeli nation. This militant group was formed in 1982 and is based in Lebanon.

Formed and aided by Ayatollah Khomeini, they spread Islamic revolution by strictly following Islamic Shi'a ideology.

*Hamas* is a Palestinian hate group that governs the Gaza Strip. An offshoot of the Egyptian Muslim brotherhood, Hamas was founded in 1987 to "liberate" Palestine from Israel.

Wars and rumors of wars will continue until an uneasy—and temporary—peace is orchestrated by the antichrist. But the Church of Jesus Christ will stand against all, for God promised in Psalm 91:14-16, *"I will save those who love Me, and will protect those who acknowledge Me as Lord. When they call to me, I will answer them; when they are in trouble, I will be with them. I will rescue them..."*

In Romans 9:18-19, Paul reminds us that God will have mercy on whom He wants to have mercy and will harden His heart against those He wants to reject. I understand that some might say this seems unfair. But Paul asks some important questions. Who are we to question God? Doesn't the Potter have the right to make what He will out of the clay? He can mold some clay for special purposes and some for common use.

The Jewish and Arab nations are constantly at war. No man can broker a lasting peace treaty. So, what issues are at the heart of the conflict?

1. Obviously, the land of Israel itself. Both Jews and Arabs claim the land. Only God can decide who owns it—and He already has.
2. Palestine: The only resolution is a spiritual one. No man can broker a solution agreeable to everyone. There will be no true peace until Jesus returns.

## CHAPTER FOUR

# THE "FOOLISHNESS" OF GOD'S MERCY

**"For the word of the cross is foolishness to those who are perishing, but to us who are being saved it is the power of God." (1 Corinthians 1:18 NASB)**

God made a promise in the Garden of Eden that He would send a Messiah to restore humankind's relationship with Himself. His own Son would take the punishment for our sin on Himself. He would suffer and die on our behalf, in our place. And that's exactly what Jesus did!

He put death to death! He paid our debt, one He did not owe, and He saved and restored us to a full relationship with God.

Sadly, Paul's words to the Corinthian Church (quoted at the beginning of this chapter) are still true today. Too many see Christ's sacrifice as foolishness.

Paul basically divided mankind into two groups: those perishing and those destined for eternity in heaven, sharing in God's glory.

Paul knew the Lord did not send him to focus on speaking eloquent words, but to focus on the cross. While Eve was deceived, Adam sinned. This may sound ridiculous to those who don't believe in Christ, but while unbelievers are facing death, they also see the futility of their lives and the hopelessness of their future.

I cannot understand why young Arab people, with their entire lives ahead of them, strap explosives to their bodies and blow themselves up to kill a few Jews. Does anyone truly understand how men can intentionally fly planes into buildings? Or how Omar Mir Seddique Mateen in June 2016 could kill 49 people and injure 53 others in a Florida nightclub?

I think the answer is that they all believed the Lie—the "I will be as God" lie—just like Lucifer. Just like Eve.

Tragically, many young people are being brainwashed, many by their parents. You see, we are all blank canvases at birth. Our beliefs are established through repetition in what we call the formative years.

## THE ORIGIN OF ISLAM:

Where and how did the Muslim religion begin? In 610 A.D. while meditating in a cave on Mount Hira, Muhammad had a "revelation" and truly believed God had spoken to him through visions. These visions formed the basis of Islam.

Muhammad's teachings met with resistance as his message threatened polytheism and the political powers of the day. The upper classes rejected him, but he did draw some followers from the lower classes. The turning point came in 622 when Muhammad moved from Mecca to Yathrib (present-day Medina). By the time Muhammad died, Islam had spread to Asia, Africa, and parts of Europe.

The basic difference between Christianity and Islam is that the God of the Christians is Love Incarnate who desires personal relationships with His creation. Allah of Islam is not personable but is considered to be transcendent and so far above his creation that he is not personally knowable.

I mentioned earlier that many young Muslims have taken their own lives as suicide bombers. Ironically, suicide is specifically forbidden by the Islamic holy book, the Quran. Since that is true, how can Islamic leaders sanction such actions?

The promise of a martyr's reward can be tempting, especially for those whose lives are less than joyful. As specified in the Quran, male martyrs receive 72 virgin maidens in paradise. Women will dwell in castles and will regain their virginity, along with unimaginable beauty. Each female martyr will be able to choose her husband, and he will remain faithful to her.

## THE ETERNAL CONFLICT

Many stories have been told and written regarding this eternal conflict between Jews and Arabs. I recently watched a dramatic a series on Netflix called *"Fauda"* (the literal meaning of this word is *chaos*).

It was written by two former IDF (Israel Defense Force) patriots, Lior Raz and Avi Issacharoff, who drew on their own experiences. *"Fauda"* is an intense thriller that reveals the hatred on both sides of the Palestinian issue. It may be a story on Netflix for most, but for those in the Middle East it is reality. As I've said, this conflict will not be resolved until the Lord Himself returns. Meanwhile, we Christians must continue to pray for the peace of Israel.

## THE ROOTS OF HATRED

Muslims have always hated non-Muslims, which, of course, includes Christians and especially Jews. Originating with Ishmael, this hate dates back thousands of years.

## The Ultimate Plague

We've already talked about Abraham, who is considered the father of the Jews, as well as the father of the Arabs. Abraham or Ibrahim (as known by the Arabs) lived in the Middle East about 4,000 years ago and had two sons. God had promised Abraham that he would become the father of many nations, that his descendants would number more than the stars in the sky, and that the Messiah would come through his lineage. As Abraham and Sarah, his wife, were both well beyond childbearing age when this promise was made, Sarah decided to help God out by urging her husband to sleep with her young Egyptian servant, Hagar. Sarah would then raise the resulting child as her own. Hagar gave birth to Ishmael, and anger and jealousy rose up between the two women.

Despite Sarah's disbelief and her advanced age, God fulfilled His promise, and she also became pregnant by Abraham and gave birth to a son, Isaac. Sarah nursed the baby herself, and, as God commanded, Isaac was circumcised on the eighth day. Abraham was one hundred years old at that time.

Tension between the women was too much for Sarah to bear. After she found Ishmael mocking Isaac (Genesis 21:9), she demanded that Abraham send Hagar and Ishmael away. While Abraham was distressed by this, God told him to honor Sarah by doing as she asked.

As the son of Abraham's true wife, Isaac would inherit Abraham's wealth (Genesis 25:1-5), but Abraham gave gifts to the sons of his concubines and sent them, including Ishmael, to settle in the East.

Ishmael had twelve sons who became *"princes according to their nations"* (Genesis 25:12-16) in fulfillment of the divine promise to Hagar that God would *"increase your descendants so much that they will be too numerous to count"* (Genesis 16:10).

In Genesis 17:20, God told Abraham that He would surely bless Ishmael.

*"I will make him fruitful and will greatly increase his numbers. He will be the father of twelve rulers, and I will make him into a great nation."*

God kept His word, and the Ishmaelites lived *"from Havilah as far as Shur, which is east of Egypt as you head to Assyria"* (Genesis 25:18) where they lived in hostility toward all the tribes related to them.

Today, the Arab peoples claim Ishmael as their ancestor, while the Jewish race follows its lineage all the way back to Isaac. They have the same father, but there is very little brotherly love between them.

CHAPTER FIVE

# THE STRUGGLE CONTINUES: THE STORY OF JACOB & ESAU

> "The Lord said to her (Rebekah), 'Two nations are in your womb, and two peoples from within you will be separated; one people will be stronger than the other, and the older will serve the younger.'" (Genesis 25:23)

When Isaac grew up, he married Rebekah, who became pregnant with twin sons, Esau and Jacob. It seems that almost from the moment of their conception, the boys were at odds with each other. The Bible says that Rebekah could feel them fighting with each other in her womb (Genesis 25:22).

According to the custom of that day, the firstborn son, Esau, would inherit two-thirds of his father's possessions. But Genesis 25:29-34 tells us that one day Jacob was cooking some stew when Esau came in from the open country, famished. He asked for some of the stew, but Jacob replied that he wanted Esau's birthright in exchange. At that point, Esau's hunger overcame his logic.

> "Look, I am about to die," Esau said. "What good is the birthright to me?" (Verse 32)

And so Esau surrendered his birthright to Jacob.

But even though Esau had given up his birthright, by custom he still should have received the blessing reserved for the firstborn son. However, it was not God's will for Esau to receive this blessing. His plan was to prosper the lineage of Abraham through the pure line of Jacob. Esau had taken two wives who were Hittites, and these wives were *"a source of grief to Isaac and Rebekah"* (Genesis 26:35).

The scripture tells us that Isaac loved Esau, but Rebekah loved Jacob. So, when Isaac was about to die (and had lost his eyesight in his old age), he called for Esau so that he might bless him. But Rebekah disguised Jacob as his older brother, and Isaac blessed him instead of Esau.

When Esau arrived to find that Jacob had stolen his blessing, he begged for a blessing from Isaac. But Isaac had already blessed Jacob and that blessing would stand. Esau asked if Isaac had reserved any blessing at all for him, and Isaac replied:

> *"'I have made him lord over you and have made all his relatives his servants, and I have sustained him with grain and new wine. So what can I possibly do for you, my son?'*
>
> *"Esau said to his father, 'Do you have only one blessing, my father? Bless me too, my father!' Then Esau wept aloud.*
>
> *"His father Isaac answered him, 'Your dwelling will be away from the earth's richness, away from the dew of heaven above. You will live by the sword and you will serve your brother. But when you grow restless, you will throw his yoke from off your neck.'"*

## The Struggle Continues: The Story Of Jacob & Esau

Esau held a grudge against Jacob because of the blessing his father had given him. He said to himself, *"The days of mourning for my father are near; then I will kill my brother Jacob"* (Genesis 27:37-41).

The prophet Malachi gives us more insight into the relationship between the Jews (the descendants of Abraham, Isaac, and Jacob) and the Arabs (the descendants of Cain, Ishmael, and Esau). When Israel doubted God's love, the word of the Lord came through Malachi:

> *"'I have loved you,' says the Lord. But you ask, 'How have you loved us?' 'Was not Esau Jacob's brother?" declares the Lord. Yet I have loved Jacob, but Esau I have hated, and I have turned his hill country into a wasteland and left his inheritance to the desert jackals'"* (Malachi 1:2-3).

We see that even from their mother's womb, God loved Jacob and hated Esau because of what they would become and what their descendants would become. The difference between the twins was clear. Esau was a cunning hunter, a man of the field, while Jacob was a plain man and dwelled in tents. Jacob was able to plan ahead and handle delayed gratification, unlike Esau who wanted immediate physical satisfaction.

Esau relocated to Mt. Seir (later called Petra by the Greeks). After removing the Horites from their 32-square-mile cave city, Esau made it the capital of his empire. Jacob, on the other hand, went northward to Hara, where he prospered.

The descendants of Esau were the Edomites who lived in a barren land of rocks and caves. My wife and I visited Petra, and I can assure you nothing green grows there. No grass, no trees, only stubble that the goats eat.

The descendants of Jacob were the Israelites, who were blessed in the land flowing in milk and honey.

Many years later, when the descendants of Jacob traveled to Egypt to find relief from a famine, they were enslaved by the Egyptians for 400 years. In what we call the Exodus, God appointed Moses to lead the Israelites out of Egypt and return to the land that had been promised to Abraham so many years before. This took place in approximately the twelfth or thirteenth century before the birth of Christ.

As you know, the Lord parted the Red Sea so the Israelites could pass through on dry land, but then brought the waters together, drowning the Egyptian soldiers who were pursuing them. After this, the Israelites had to travel through Edomite territory to reach the Promised Land. But the Edomites (descendants of Esau) refused to let them pass through. Not only did they object to letting the Israelites cross through, they actually wanted to kill them. This hatred had been handed down from previous generations who resented Jacob, the one who they believed had stolen their birthright and their blessing.

The Bible pictures the Edomites as a warlike people, an angry, deceitful and treacherous race who sold their captives into slavery. Their raiding parties from Petra pillaged Israelite villages and killed as many inhabitants as possible.

Finally, King David had enough. He waged war with the Edomites and placed garrisons in Edom to keep the peace (1 Chronicles 18:13). These incursions would resume when King Solomon, against God's warnings, married Edomite women. Israel retaliated after each incursion, similarly to what is happening today between the Palestinians and Jews.

In 800 BC King Amaziah killed ten thousand Edomites in the Valley of Salt and then took ten thousand Edomites back to Petra and threw them off the high cliffs (2 Kings 14:7).

In 600 BC the Edomites made a mutual-assist treaty with the Babylonians and assisted them in destroying Jerusalem. It was common practice, in those days, to racially integrate conquered nations, thereby destroying the will to reoccupy their land. The most learned Jews and best physical specimens were taken. The Edomites moved from Petra to Jerusalem, then the Nabateans (descendants of Ishmael) moved from Arabia to inhabit Petra.

When the Romans invaded the Middle East, Israel once again found themselves under the tyranny of a foreign government. The Romans would not put an Israeli in charge and instead selected Idumeans (Edomites), known as the Herods, to supervise police and civil activities. During the destruction of Jerusalem in 70 A.D., Jews were either killed, sold into slavery, or fled to other countries. The Edomites stayed because they had nothing to fear from the Romans. They became the ancestors of the present-day Palestinians.

Josephus, a Roman-Jewish first-century historian, wrote that the Idumeans spared no one and that they were a most barbarous and bloody nation. He also noted that the Edomites hated the Jews and recorded that "this hatred, when unleashed, knew no reason or bounds."[5]

The confederacy formed against Israel emphasized that they were not only against Israel but against Yahweh, the God of Israel. The Psalmist in Psalm 83 listed ten nations in a coalition led by Moab and Ammon who stand against Israel. (Ammon is present-day Jordan; Moab is located east of the Dead Sea in what is now west-central Jordan.)

This same hate exists today between the Jews and the Arabs and between the Palestinians and the Jews. It has

---

[5] Wars of the Jews. Book #4 chapter 5

manifested in all parts of the world, and, tragically, will continue until the Lord returns.

The Bible is clear that Israel will prevail in the end—not because of their might, but because God will always protect them.

## CHAPTER SIX

# ISRAEL: THE CENTER OF THE WORLD?

*"I lift up my eyes to the mountains—
where does my help come from?
My help comes from the LORD,
the Maker of heaven and earth.
He will not let your foot slip—
he who watches over you will not slumber;
indeed, he who watches over Israel
will neither slumber nor sleep."*
**(Psalm 121:1-4)**

Rarely does a day go by that we do not hear or read about Israel in the news. It seems that the words of the prophet Zechariah have come to pass:

> *"And in that day will I make Jerusalem a burdensome stone for all people; all that burden themselves with it shall be cut in pieces, though all the people of the earth be gathered against it"* (Zechariah 12:3).

As we've said, the nations of the world have always hated Israel. While Jerusalem means "habitation of peace," it is one of the most violent cities in the world. My wife and I spent three weeks visiting Jerusalem several years ago. It was disconcerting to see Israelis who were in the IDF (Israel Defense Forces) carrying guns on the streets.

The devil has been trying to kill the Jews for thousands of years because he knows God loves them. He knows they are the chosen people. He thinks if he can eradicate the Jews, he can change the game. Mere man cannot thwart the devil's actions, only God can do that. Therefore, all the well-meaning presidents and other dignitaries who continue to orchestrate plans for peace will always be frustrated.

Humanity's simple plan should be to follow and trust the Lord. One of the first promises God made to man (Abraham) is, *"I will make you into a great nation and I will bless you; I will make your name great, and you will be a blessing. I will bless those who bless you, and whoever curses you I will curse; and all peoples on earth will be blessed through you"* (Genesis 12:1-3 emphasis mine). If you truly love the Lord, you should never curse Israel. If you hate the people of Israel, you, in turn, are hating the God of Israel.

Many people have asked me why I believe as I do. The answer is found in John 8:32: *"You shall know the truth, and the truth shall make you free."* The real question they want answered is how I can be so sure the Bible and, specifically, Bible prophecy is correct. To answer this question, I must begin with why God gives us prophecy in the first place.

Prophecy is one of the best proofs that the Bible is true and that it was written by men who were inspired by the Holy Spirit. For instance, Daniel predicted the existence of every world power from his day until ours.

One fifth of the Bible is prophetic. Dr. Peter Stoner, a math professor and author, did a study on fulfilled prophecy. Dr.

Stoner is probably best known for his book, *"Science Speaks,"*[6] in which he discusses Bible prophecies in relation to calculations and probability estimates.

Stoner considered the prophet Micah who in 700 B.C. prophesied that the Messiah would be born in Bethlehem. The prophet Malachi (400 years before Christ's birth) predicted that the Messiah would have a forerunner (John the Baptist). Zechariah prophesied that the Messiah would be betrayed by a friend, sold for thirty pieces of silver, and that the money would be used to buy a potters' (or debtors') field.

Dr. Stoner chose eleven such prophecies. The odds of just these eleven prophesies being fulfilled by one man are 1 to 1,000.000,000,000,000,000,000,000,000 or one out of a septillion! Jesus fulfilled over 300 of these prophecies. What do you think the odds are? The resulting number is impossible for us to read, according to our most powerful computer. Second Corinthians 1:20 (NKJV) proclaims, *"For all the promises of God in Him are Yes, and in Him Amen, to the glory of God through us."*

Bible prophecies are the promises of God. The Living Bible (paraphrase) says it this way:

> *"He carries out and fulfills all of God's promises, no matter how many of them there are; and we have told everyone how faithful He is, giving glory to His name"* (2 Corinthians 1:20).

The Bible, as inspired by the Holy Spirit, is without error. Second Timothy 3:16-17 (NKJV) tells us,

---

[6] http://sciencespeaks.dstoner.net/

*"All Scripture is given by inspiration of God, and is profitable for doctrine, for reproof, for correction, for instruction in righteousness, that the man of God may be complete, thoroughly equipped for every good work."*

With the above in mind, consider this: Which nations have reappeared on the world stage two thousand years after being captured by another nation? Only one. Israel.

One factor that allowed ancient Rome to grow and prosper was its ability to assimilate other cultures. The Romans would first install a small militia group to oversee daily operations and arbitrate disputes. Then they would carry out an exchange of populations, where a certain number of men and women would be shipped from the conquered land to Rome and an equal number of Romans would be shipped to the conquered land. Before long, the conquered countries had adopted Roman culture and spoke the language of the conqueror.

But there was a very important exception to this: Israel. The Jews refused to intermarry or adopt the customs and language of Rome, thereby retaining the purity of the nation.

Moses prophesied that the Jewish nation would be exiled but, after many years, would be regathered from the nations.

> *"And the Lord your God, will bring you to the land which your forefathers possessed, and you will take possession of it, and He will do good to you, and He will make you more numerous than your forefathers"* (Deuteronomy 30:5).

Another relevant verse can be found in Amos 9:8:

> *"'Yet I will not totally destroy the descendants of Jacob,' declares the Lord."* Verse 15 adds, *"'I will plant Israel in*

*their own land, never again to be uprooted from the land I have given them,' says the Lord your God."*

Therefore, even a miracle as momentous as the Exodus is dwarfed next to the re-birth of the Israeli nation.

*"And it shall come to pass in that day, that the Lord shall set his hand again the second time to recover the remnant of His people, which shall be left from Assyria* [present-day Turkey and northern Iraq] *and Egypt and from Pathros* [present-day Northern Africa] *and from Cush,* [Ethiopia] *and from Elam* [Iran] *and from Shinar* [Niffer] *and from Hamath* [about 60 miles southeast of Babylon] **and from the islands of the sea**" [most likely a reference to England, America, Australia, Japan, Korea] (Isaiah 11:11 KJV *notations mine*).

God reaffirmed what He told Isaiah in Jeremiah 16:14,15:

*"'However, the days are coming,' declares the Lord, 'when it will no longer be said, 'As surely as the Lord lives, who brought the Israelites up out of Egypt,' but it will be said, 'As surely as the Lord lives, who brought the Israelites up out of the land of the north and out of all the countries where he had banished them.' For I will restore them to the land I gave their ancestors.'"*

This is an amazing prophecy. The Jews viewed the Exodus as the greatest event in their history, but Jeremiah said there would be something greater: the return of the Jews to their land.

This re-birth took place in 1948. Of the approximately fifteen million Jews in the world today, nine million reside in Israel. Of that number only about two percent are Christians.

Repossessing the land was indeed a major miracle. Two thousand years had elapsed since Jerusalem fell to the

Romans and the citizens of Israel dispersed to the nations. Not only did they return to the land the Lord had given to Abraham, but they returned speaking their own Hebrew language, keeping all their traditions, and rebuilding a land that was filled with swamps, mosquitos, and wild animals, including lions, bears, antelope, ostriches, and crocodiles.

In a quote from *The Weekly Standard*, May 11, 1998, Charles Krauthammer said, "Israel is the very embodiment of Jewish continuity: It is the only nation on earth that inhabits the same land, bears the same name, speaks the same language, and worships the same God that it did 3,000 years ago. You dig the soil, and you find pottery from Davidic times, coins from Bar Kokhba, and 2,000-year-old scrolls written in a script remarkably like the one that today advertises ice cream at the corner candy store."[7]

Life was very diffcult for the returning Jews. The Hula swamps were drained in northern Israel to create farmland, making the deserts bloom. The idea of turning mosquito-infested swamps into farmland was foremost on the domestic front. After the swamps were drained, according to Changan Dimentman, an ecologist at the Hebrew University, flooding would occur seasonally, thus sending nourishing nitrates and phosphorus into the Sea of Galilee.[8] Algae exploded.

Rabinovitz (a Kibbutz leader) remarked concerning the re-flooding project that draining the Hula swamps was not a mistake. He says he has a way to improve the soil by spraying manganese.

---

[7] https://www.science.co.il/israel-history/

[8] https://www.newscientist.com/article/mg13818691-400-israel-floods-drained-swamp-to-bring-in-tourists/

## A HISTORY OF CRUELTY

Matthew 2:16 shows us how cruel the Edomites could be. King Herod ordered the murder of all male children in Jerusalem and surrounding areas. This type of response from Herod was not unexpected, as he also had his wife and two sons killed.

The Palestinian Liberation Organization (PLO) was founded in 1964 with its stated goal being the "liberation of Palestine" through armed struggle.[9] In other words, they want to take back the land Israel repossessed in 1948. Chairman Yasser Arafat's action plan was to kill as many Jews and Americans as he could by any means. His life ended in 2004 at the age of 75. While there were many theories of how he died, most agree he was poisoned.[10]

Over 1,375 people have been killed by Palestinian violence and terrorism since September 2000.[11] This is another example of the deep hatred of Esau's descendants, whose ideology is deeply rooted in the Palestinians.

The eventual fate of the Edomites (Palestinians) can be found in Ezekiel 35:1-2, 4-5:

*"The word of the Lord came to me: 'Son of man, set your face against Mt. Seir; prophesy against it and say: This is what the sovereign Lord says: 'I am against you, Mt. Seir, and I*

---

[9] "Permanent Observer Mission of Palestine to the United Nations – Palestine National Charter of 1964". 30 November 2010. Archived from the original on 30 November 2010. Retrieved 8 March 2017.

[10] https://www.britannica.com/biography/Yasser-Arafat/From-agreement-to-the-second-intifadah

[11] https://www.mfa.gov.il/mfa/foreignpolicy/terrorism/palestinian/pages/victims

*will stretch out my hand against you and make you a desolate waste. I will turn your towns into ruins and you will be desolate. Then you will know that I am the Lord.*

*"'Because you harbored an ancient hostility and delivered the Israelites over to the sword at the time of their calamity, the time their punishment reached its climax, therefore as surely as I live,' declares the sovereign Lord, 'I will give you over to bloodshed and it will pursue you. I will make Mt. Seir a desolate waste and cut off from all that come and go.'"*

Verse nine says it best: *"I will make you desolate forever; your towns will not be inhabited. Then you will know that I am the Lord."*

The ongoing struggle between the Israelis and the Arabs still comes down to who has a right to the land. Before that question can be answered, there are issues that must be resolved regarding authority and rights.

Rights are a major issue in today's world. The rights of nations. The rights of individuals. The rights of minority groups and religious groups. Transgender and homosexual rights. The basic right to human dignity and property.

Is there true authority without morality? Is it really true that "might makes right"? Is true authority found on the side of whoever is richest or the strongest? The real question is, "What makes anything right or wrong?"

The answer is God.

He is the only true source of authority. He sets the rules and determines rights. Authority and morality exist because God exists. *"Let everyone be subject to the governing authorities, for there is no authority except that which God has established"* (Romans 13:1).

God Almighty has already established the rights of Israel to own the land she currently occupies. Leviticus 25:23 tells us all land belongs to God *("...for the land is Mine, for you are but aliens and sojourners with Me")*, and that God gave the land to the descendants of Abraham (see Genesis 12:7, 13:15, and 15:18).

In Genesis 17:7-8, the Lord reaffirmed His covenant. The sign of that covenant for Abraham and his descendants was circumcision.

It's important to understand that the promise of the land was not based or dependent upon Israel's character or faithfulness. The covenant was based solely on God's grace and secured by His oath

As we established earlier, the promise to Abraham's descendants does not include Ishmael and his descendants, but is solely for Isaac and his lineage (Genesis 17:18).

The New Testament agrees in Hebrews 11:18, saying, *"In Isaac your descendants shall be called."* Nor was the land given to the other sons of Abraham. Genesis 25:5-6 says,

> *"Now Abraham gave all he had to Isaac, but to the sons of the concubines, Abraham gave gifts while he was still living, and sent them away from his son Isaac eastward, to the land of the east."*

When Jacob was about to die, he told his sons,

> *"God will surely take care of you, and bring you up from this land* [Egypt] *to the land which He promised on oath to Abraham, to Isaac and to Jacob* (Genesis 50:24 notation mine)."

But what about the many times when the Children of Israel wandered away from God and worshipped idols? Why didn't God punish them and withdraw His promise?

The answer lies in Leviticus 26:40-45, where the Lord assures Israel that He will bring them back from their wanderings, from their captivity. The land was a gift bestowed upon Israel, and their sin and dispersion did not alter God's plan nor change their divine right to the land.

About 2,700 years ago, the prophet Ezekiel spoke of "dry bones" in describing the restoration of Israel in the last days. As mentioned previously, no other nation in history has miraculously been restored, retaining their original language and customs.

> *"Then he said to me: 'Son of man, these bones are the people of Israel. They say, 'Our bones are dried up and our hope is gone; we are cut off.' Therefore prophesy and say to them: 'This is what the Sovereign Lord says: My people, I am going to open your graves and bring you up from them; I will bring you back to the land of Israel'"* (Ezekiel 37:11-12).

## THE MIRACULOUS RESTORATION OF ISRAEL

The rebirth of Israel was a miracle.

When studying prophecy regarding end times, one of the first signs of the imminence of Christ's return is Israel's re-birth. After over two thousand years of being scattered over the entire earth, those "dry bones" are now coming home.

At one time, Israel was ruled by the Persians, then the Greeks, and then by the Romans. As Rome began to fall apart, the Ottoman Empire took control of Palestine. Then the British outmuscled the Ottoman Empire, continuing the subjection by foreigners of the land called Palestine.

Isaiah prophesied in Isaiah 66:7-8,

*"Before she goes into labor, she gives birth; before the pains come upon her, she delivers a son. Who has ever heard of such things? Who has ever seen things like this? Can a country be born in a day or a nation be brought forth in a moment? Yet no sooner is Zion in labor than she gives birth to her children."*

The Bible foretold that the restoration of Israel would be amazing. It was indeed born in one day, and birth pangs did not occur until five days after the birth of the restored Israeli nation. That was when five Arab nations attacked Israel.

The first war was a War of Independence, followed by the Suez Crisis of 1956. The Six-Day War in 1967 was followed by the War of Attrition ('67 to '70), which involved fighting between Egypt, Jordan, and the PLO. The Yom Kippur War in 1973 was followed by a series of wars with the Palestinians.

But no one has overtaken Israel.

Psalm 91:9-11 tells us,

**"Because thou hast made the Lord, which is my refuge, even the most High thy habitation, there shall no evil befall thee, neither shall any plague come near thy dwelling, for he shall give his angels charge over thee, to keep thee in all thy ways" (KJV).**

# CHAPTER SEVEN

# WHAT DOES ALL THIS HAVE TO DO WITH YOU?

As you've been reading through this book, you may have been thinking, "This is all interesting, but what does it have to do with me?"

If so, I want you to know that just as God has a plan for the nation and people of Israel, He has a plan for you as well. Just as He has preserved and kept Israel over the centuries – even bringing their dry bones to life again after the world thought they were dead and scattered to the winds, He will preserve everything that you commit to Him forever. Not a single hair on your head will be lost if you trust in Him and commit yourself to Him.

When you go to your grave, the world may think you are gone forever. But, if you belong to Jesus, that will not be true. Like Israel, you will be resurrected and restored when Jesus comes to reign over the earth. And I am convinced that all those who rise from the dead will be restored to perfection. Those who were blind on earth will have 20/20 vision. Those who were crippled will run and jump like Olympic athletes. The deaf will be able to hear their loved ones' voices. Those whose minds were ravaged by Alzheimer's disease will have all their memories restored. This is the future that awaits those who have surrendered their lives to Jesus! We will finally be who our Creator intended us to be, free from the imperfections this fallen world imposes on us.

Once you realize that there really is a God, a God who loves you, a God who protects you, a God who wants a personal relationship with you, then and only then will you be truly protected. I am an old man these days, but I want to share some of my elderly wisdom. Parents who allow their children to be taken in by the transgender and gay agenda will one day stand in front of a just God and give an account for their actions.

I ask two questions: Can God make a mistake? What is your definition of sin?

Answering the first question is simple. Malachi 3:6 tells us, *"I the Lord do not change."* God is unchanging in His character. God is pure Spirit whose being is all wisdom, all powerful, all goodness, all holiness, all justice, and all trustworthy as He is the Truth.

Other references attesting to our unchanging God include,

> *"He who is the Glory of Israel does not lie or change his mind; for he is not a human being, that he should change his mind"* (1 Samuel 15:29).

> *"God, who is enthroned from of old, who does not change—he will hear them and humble them, because they have no fear of God"* (Psalm 55:19).

> *"Every good and perfect gift is from above, coming down from the Father of the heavenly lights, who does not change like shifting shadows"* (James 1:17).

God is perfect. There are many scriptures proclaiming His perfection. *"As for God, His way is blameless; The word of the Lord is refined; He is a shield to all who take refuge in Him"* (Psalm 18:30 NASB). The New International Version reads,*"...as for God His way is perfect..."*

Hebrews 13:8 reminds us that *"Jesus Christ is the same yesterday and today and forever."*

Because God is all knowing, He cannot be unaware of anything and knows what will happen before it happens.

Some question God's unchanging and perfect nature when reading Genesis 6:6, which states, *"And it repented the Lord that he had made man on the earth, and it grieved him at his heart"* (KJV). Other versions say that the Lord regretted making man (or was sorry).

When the Bible speaks of God repenting, being sorry, or regretting, it doesn't mean God changed His mind. These verses should be regarded as a metaphorical description of God's actions over His creation. God is said to regret only by comparison to humans who are filled with regret.

This scripture does not imply any uneasiness in God, for nothing or no one can disturb His eternal mind. This speaks more to His hate for sin and His heart for mankind. God was pleased with the work of His hand, His creation, but He was displeased with man after the fall. The change was in man and not God. God cannot make a mistake.

But as Timothy wrote: *"For the time will come when they will not endure sound doctrine; but after their own lusts shall they heap to themselves teachers, having itching ears; and they shall turn away their ears from the truth, and shall be turned unto fables"* (2 Timothy 4:3).

Most people try to reason with God as if He were like man in His thinking. We say things like, "Surely, God will understand." "God wants me to be happy." "God knows my heart."

"Surely, God is okay with men and women who simply live together."

"Surely, it's okay to have a gay relationship and gay marriage, as long as there's love. After all, He made me this way, so He must see my lifestyle as acceptable."

"Because I'm divorced (or widowed) surely God doesn't mind if I have a sexual encounter every once in a while."

The truth of the matter is that God is not like man. He is totally, completely holy. There is no sin in Him, and He cannot look on or abide sin.

In God's eyes, sin is sin. There are no small or venial sins. You don't get a nod for a little white lie. And the Scripture is clear that if you break one commandment, one law, you are guilty of breaking them all.

*"For whoever keeps the whole law and yet stumbles at just one point is guilty of breaking all of it"* (James 2:10).

Romans 3: 23 tells us everyone sins. No one is perfect. *"...for all have sinned and fall short of the glory of God,"* and Romans 6:23 details the consequences of sin and of holiness attained through Jesus. *"For the wages of sin is death, but the gift of God is eternal life in Christ Jesus our Lord."* Indeed, without the saving power of Jesus Christ, all those who sin (and that would be everyone) are condemned to eternity in hell.

Our God is truly all knowing.

*"Great is our Lord and mighty in power; his understanding has no limit"* (Psalm 147:5).

*"Even if we feel guilty, God is greater than our feelings, and he knows everything"* (1 John 3:20).

Hebrews 4:13 (NLT) records,

*"Nothing in all creation is hidden from God. Everything is naked and exposed before his eyes, and he is the one to whom we are accountable."*

These are but a few passages that show us that God is all knowing and all powerful. He cannot make mistakes, and man is accountable to Him. He cannot change His mind because His will has no limits and is eternal.

God Almighty Himself decided our gender. He commanded us in Genesis 1:28 to be fruitful and multiply. Same-sex unions are incapable of fulfilling this command and, therefore, cannot be blessed by God.

Are you wondering why your prayers seem to go unanswered? Are you encountering problem after problem in your life, but your continual reaching out to God feels in vain? We answer to a holy God, and holiness is the key to communicating with Him. Sin and unbelief block the blessings of the Lord.

While Christians are not perfect, we are in the process of sanctification, growing daily to become more and more like Christ. Non-Christians, however, are lost and separated from God by sin. Christ's death on the cross—and His victory over that death—allowed man the ability to speak to God directly without having to go through a priest or other religious leader.

Man's pride forms a wall between God and man. We all hate to admit we are sinners. But, as noted earlier, we all have sinned and fall short of the glory of God because of that sin.

As an aside to my Catholic brothers and sisters, "all" includes Mary, the mother of Jesus. In her Magnificat in Luke 1:46-55, she says, *"My soul glorifies the Lord and my spirit rejoices in God my Savior, for he has been mindful of the humble state of his servant."* Only those who need to be saved need a Savior (which is everyone). Mary recognized her own humble state.

Most of us rationalize our sin. The question isn't whether we have sinned (we have and we do), but if we will acknowledge this sin and understand that, when we choose sin, we also choose God as our enemy. If we want answers to our questions, answers to our prayers—if we want to see God move in our lives—then we must repent. We must confess our sinfulness to God, asking for forgiveness, and receive the sacrifice of the blood of Jesus to cover that sin. Accepting Christ as Savior brings us God's forgiveness and sets our feet on the right path.

> *"If we confess our sins, he is faithful and just and will forgive us our sins and purify us from all unrighteousness"* (1 John 1:9).

> *"For the eyes of the Lord are on the righteous and his ears are attentive to their prayer, but the face of the Lord is against those who do evil"* (1 Peter 3:12).

Do you have any interest in God's will? Do you pray and feel like it's a waste of time? Perhaps you pray, but pray in doubt. Perhaps you look somewhere else for answers because you're not sure God is coming through for you. This attitude leads to more frustration. God set the ground rules. When we follow those rules, we succeed.

## THE PHARISEE AND THE TAX COLLECTOR

To some who were confident of their own righteousness and looked down on everyone else, Jesus told this parable:

*"Two men went up to the temple to pray, one a Pharisee and the other a tax collector. The Pharisee stood by himself and prayed: 'God, I thank you that I am not like other people—robbers, evildoers, adulterers—or even like this tax collector. I fast twice a week and give a tenth of all I get.'*

*"But the tax collector stood at a distance. He would not even look up to heaven, but beat his breast and said, 'God, have mercy on me, a sinner.'*

*"I tell you that this man, rather than the other, went home justified before God. For all those who exalt themselves will be humbled, and those who humble themselves will be exalted."*

In this passage in Luke 18:9-14, we see two different attitudes, two different approaches to sin. The vain and proud Pharisee boasted to God of all he had done. In his arrogance, he proclaimed himself to be sin-free. The tax collector stood at a distance, unable to look up, and confessed his sinfulness, asking for mercy. Jesus described the resulting consequences saying that those who exalt themselves will be humbled, and those who humble themselves will be exalted.

If you were to ask people to give you the definition of sin, you would most likely be surprised at the number of people who are in the dark. They may make a feeble attempt to answer but will probably fall far short of the truth.

## AN INCREASE IN UNBELIEF

A Pew Report survey conducted in 2018 and 2019 showed that four percent of American adults claim to be atheists, up from two percent in 2009. An additional five percent of

Americans call themselves agnostics, up from three percent a decade ago.[12]

Atheists make up a larger share of the population in many European countries than they do in the United States, with nineteen percent of Belgians identifying as atheist, sixteen percent in Denmark, fifteen percent in France, and fourteen percent in the Netherlands and Sweden. Other countries stack up this way: Spain at eight percent, Switzerland at eight percent, and Italy at six percent, Surprisingly, only four percent of Russians claim to be atheists, while the Czech Republic has the highest rate at twenty-five percent.

I think it's interesting to note that over two-thirds of atheists are male with an average age of 34. Most are well educated and align themselves with the Democratic Party and liberalism.

Like the majority of Americans, most Atheists consider family to be the source of meaning in their lives.

Atheists and, I venture to say, agnostics, consider sin as a theological concept, while Christians understand sin as "missing the mark," an immoral act that transgresses God's laws. Sin is a consequence of Adam's transgression in the Garden of Eden. That transgression is passed on through what is now known as man's sin nature.

Because of man's sin nature, sinning became natural. Man looks only to what can make him happy or feels good. Sin nature is that part of man that causes him to rebel against God. In other words, we have a natural inclination to sin, a desire to gratify the flesh. "Wine, women, and song" is sin nature's anthem. Consider that we do not have to teach children to lie or to be selfish. Sinning is natural, a part of the fabric of humanity.

---

[12] https://www.pewresearch.org/fact-tank/2019/12/06/10-facts-about-atheists/

Romans 6:6 speaks to the body ruled by sin:

*"We know that our old sinful selves were crucified with Christ so that sin might lose its power in our lives. We are no longer slaves to sin."*

New birth—being born again—gives us the ability to reject sin. While the devil brings pressure on us to urge us to sin, we have a way of escape. James 4:7 (NKJV) instructs us to *"Therefore submit to God. Resist the devil and he will flee from you."*

Many Christians think all they need to do is recite a little prayer to get their free pass to eternity with the Lord. It's not the prayer that gets you an invitation. It's understanding, believing, and receiving what God did in Jesus that redeems us.

How can someone believe in, let alone trust, a God they don't know? It's true that He loves us all, but it's also true that He makes no exceptions. There is a difference between knowing Him and knowing about Him. Not knowing Him will one day lead to His declaration, *"Then I will tell them plainly, 'I never knew you. Away from me, you evildoers!"* (Matthew 7:23 NIV)

Near the close of the Sermon on the Mount, Jesus again contrasts two ways of life: the broad and narrow roads one must choose.

*"Enter through the narrow gate. For wide is the gate and broad is the road that leads to destruction, and many enter through it. But small is the gate and narrow the road that leads to life, and only a few find it"* (Matthew 7:13-14).

On that final day when we stand in front of Jesus awaiting His judgment on our lives, some will be admitted to the glories of heaven while others will be turned away.

Some of those who are denied entrance into heaven will be asking why. They will try to justify themselves by saying, "Didn't we preach the Word? Didn't we help the poor?" Some may point to miracles they performed or demons they kicked out in Jesus' name. But Jesus will say, "Depart from Me. I never knew you."

When your life is spent on the wide road, you may do good things, but these works, when done for your own glory and satisfaction, are nothing more than "filthy rags" (Isaiah 64:6) in the eyes of the Lord. Just as faith without works is dead, works without faith are worthless.

Those who will be ushered into heaven will be those who have abandoned themselves to God's mercy and have walked the narrow road in relationship with Him and in obedience to His will.

# CHAPTER EIGHT

# LIFE, DEATH, AND EVERYTHING IN BETWEEN

**"But in your hearts revere Christ as Lord. Always be prepared to give an answer to everyone who asks you to give the reason for the hope that you have. But do this with gentleness and respect..." (1 Peter 3:15)**

Most of us have asked at one time or another, "God, if You're up there, what do You want from me?" "If You're up there" is basically saying, "God, if You really exist, give me a sign."

The reality is that we must have faith. Most Christians identify the Bible as their source for belief. Saying that to an atheist is like saying you can drive your car to the moon. It makes no sense to him.

But if we want to be right with God, we must acknowledge the accuracy and truth found in the Bible. The many prophecies that have been fulfilled and the life lessons explained will support your beliefs. The Bible is real because of God, not the other way around. The Bible does not prove that God exists, but it proceeds on the understanding that you instinctively and naturally know there is a God.

*"For since the creation of the world God's invisible qualities—his eternal power and divine nature—have been clearly seen, being understood from what has been made, so that people are without excuse"* (Romans 1:20).

Jason Inman, in his article, *"How to Prove God Is Real, Or At Least to Stop Doing the Opposite,"* said it best: "Words can share our ideology, but only through humble works can we fully share our theology."[13] This goes hand in hand with 1 Peter 3:16:

*"Having a good conscience, so that when you are slandered, those who revile your good behavior in Christ may be put to shame."*

Therefore, according to Christ's half-brother James, the burden of proof is in our actions, not our words. Actions truly do speak louder than words. We testify that God is real by living out His words in our actions.

The question as to what God wants us to do is answered in Micah 6, which paints a picture of a courtroom with Israel as the defendant and God as the Prosecutor. The Lord has a complaint against His people and is bringing His case against Israel. God relates how He delivered them from bondage and brought them out of Egypt. God did nothing but good and was repaid with rejection and rebellion.

In this imagined courtroom, the people of Israel then shout out to God and say, "What do You want from me?" They say that nothing will satisfy Him no matter what they do. He would not be satisfied with thousands of rams or rivers

---

[13] https://finds.life.church/1-way-prove-god-real-least-stop-opposite/

of oil. In other words, they saw God as unreasonable. The Israeli nation was blinded by God's goodness.

The prophet Micah replies,

*"He has shown you, O man, what is good; And what does the Lord require of you but to do justly, to love mercy, and to walk humbly with your God"* (Micah 6:8 NKJV).

God stops all the shouting by telling His people *to do justly*—treat people as you would like to be treated. *To love mercy*—offer others the same kind of mercy you have received. And *to walk humbly with your God*. Humility must be in your heart. Remember who you serve and spend each day in close relationship with Him.

Now that we know what God wants from mankind, let's read Proverbs 6:16-19 (NKJV) to see what He hates.

*"These six things the Lord hates, yes, seven are an abomination to Him: A proud look, a lying tongue, hands that shed innocent blood, a heart that devises wicked plans, feet that are swift in running to evil, a false witness who speaks lies, and one who sows discord among brethren."*

Why does the passage start off saying that God hates six things, and then adds a seventh? Why not simply say seven? This is a common Hebrew literary pattern, a stylized way to introduce the ideas. It sometimes implies that the seventh item is a culmination or summary of the first six.[14] Let's take a closer look at these things that God hates:

---

[14] https://www.bibleref.com/Proverbs/6/Proverbs-6-16.html

- **A Proud Look.** We've all heard the expression that the eyes are the windows of the soul. While many attribute the origin of the saying to Shakespeare, you can find a precursor in Matthew 6:22-23 (NKJV).

*"The Lamp of the body is the eye. If therefore your eye is good, your whole body will be full of light. But if your eye is bad, your whole body will be full of darkness. If therefore the light that is in you is darkness, how great is that darkness."*

If our eyes are directed toward heavenly things, light is brought to our lives. But when we are double-minded, it's as if our whole body is full of darkness because we're trying to live in both worlds at the same time. Our selfish ways will control all we think or do.

- **A Lying Tongue.** We should never make a statement that isn't true or is intended to deceive. *"Lying lips are an abomination to the Lord, but those who deal trustfully are His delight"* (Proverbs 12:22 KJV). God does not give truth, He *is* truth.

Jesus told the Pharisees,

*"You belong to your father, the devil, and you want to carry out your father's desires. He was a murderer from the beginning, not holding to the truth, for there is no truth in him. When he lies, he speaks his native language, for he is a liar and the father of lies"* (John 8:44).

Satan is indeed a murderer, as his goal for every lie is death. In other words, he wants man to be destroyed. The devil and his demons pursue us every day. We must always remember and consider 1 Peter 5:8 (NLT):

> *"Stay alert! Watch out for your great enemy, the devil. He prowls around like a roaring lion, looking for someone to devour."*

In our world today, lying is often considered to be no big deal. We often refer to "little white lies," as though that term lessens the sin. Satan has deceived many into thinking that truth isn't important. He has further convinced people that there is no such thing as absolute truth. And if absolute truth does not exist, then there can be no absolute lie.

Satan can easily confuse man. Remember how he manipulated Eve in the Garden of Eden telling her she would be equal to God if she knew good and evil. Her reward for eating the fruit was death.

- **Hands That Shed Innocent Blood.** This sin obviously includes the abortion of innocent babies in the womb. I believe the United States is prophesied in Jeremiah 19:4: *"...and they have filled this place with the blood of the innocent."*

God hates the shedding of innocent blood, and the voices of millions of aborted babies cry out to Him. The blood of these innocents is on our hands. All life is sacred to God. We are more valuable than all the gold in the world. Man has value because God created us and saved us by sacrificing His own Son.

This same value is in an unborn child.

*"For you created my inmost being; you knit me together in my mother's womb. I praise you because I am fearfully and wonderfully made; your works are wonderful; I know that full well. My frame was not hidden from you when I was made in the secret place, when I was woven together in the depths of the earth"* (Psalm 139:13-16).

Our God knows our lives from beginning to end. He knows our fingerprints, with no two being the same. He planned our DNA, the color of our skin, the color of our eyes, and the gifts He would give us.

*"For we are God's handiwork, created in Christ Jesus to do good works, which God prepared in advance for us to do"* (Ephesians 2:10).

If God hates the killing of innocents (and He does), why do we not speak up? Why do we remain silent? Too often we think our one vote won't make a difference, therefore we do nothing. We must remember that "The only thing necessary for the triumph of evil is for good men to do nothing" (Edmund Burke).

- **A Heart That Devises Wicked Plans.** *"The Lord does not look at the things people look at. People look at the outward appearance, but the Lord looks at the heart"* (1 Samuel 16:7). We can't hide anything from God. While we may be able to smile and disguise our true motives to others, God sees through our facades. Our masks and veils may deceive others, but God knows our very hearts.

Scripture is very clear that *"A haughty look, a proud heart, and the plowing of the wicked are sin"* (Proverbs 21:4). Dr. Bill

Edgar, former chair of the Geneva College Board of Trustees, former Geneva College President and longtime pastor in the Reformed Presbyterian Church of North America, wrote an article on Proverbs 21:4 for Geneva College.[15] In this article, he reminds us that we stand before God as equals. Looking down one's nose at people defies God who made both the poor and the rich. Therefore, God hates a haughty look.

Arrogance such as this proceeds from a proud heart. Pride exalts itself instead of God. In the Garden, Satan lied to Eve when he promised exaltation, not humility. He told her she would be like God.

The "plowing" referred to in Proverbs 21:4 is thought to indicate that evil infects all of an evil man's works, even something as simple as plowing.

Man's "heart" in scripture defines the whole man and includes motives, desires, and thoughts. Proverbs 4:20-23 reminds us to *"...give attention to my words; Incline your ear to my sayings. Do not let them depart from your eyes; Keep them in the midst of your heart; For they are life to those who find them, And health to all their flesh. Keep your heart with all diligence, for out of it spring the issues of life."*

We must guard our actions and our speech and always be ready to forgive. Stress often resurrects old habits. While these actions, these habits, are observable by others, what about the unseen, down-deep baggage we carry?

Often when we're dating, we put on our best behavior, our "Sunday clothes." We want the other person to see the best in us. At some point, however, the hidden debris will arise. We use the phrase "the honeymoon is over" when the dark reality of who we truly are is revealed.

---

[15] https://www.geneva.edu/blog/biblical-wisdom/proverbs-21-4

In Jeremiah 17:9 (NKJV), we read, *"The heart is deceitful above all things, and desperately wicked; who can know it?"*

When everything is going well, it's easy to be thoughtful, kind, and giving. But when stress is added to our day, we too often revert to the carnal side of our natures. (Think road rage as an example.)

These problems of the heart are deep seeded and reveal themselves when least expected, but your wife or husband and peers see you as you truly are. The Lord wants us to keep cleaning out the debris in our lives. This is a constant process. The more you clean, the brighter the picture.

We must not dwell on thoughts that are not godly. Proverbs 23:6-8 tells us that our thought life reveals and determines who we are. *"For as he thinks in his heart, so is he."* It's important to remember to clean the rubbish from our minds daily. Martin Luther said, "You cannot keep birds from flying over your head, but you can keep them from building a nest in your hair."

Demons may be stronger than men, but by no means are they stronger than God. The devil will not quit. He will flee when we submit ourselves to the Lord and resist him, but he will return. We must turn our thought life over to the Holy Spirit, building our relationship with Him and making it stronger by asking the Lord for help. We were built to depend on God, so talk with Him daily.

- **Feet that are swift in running to evil.** Solomon's point here is we must deal swiftly with the evil our hearts consider. Sin is birthed in the heart, and the feet run in pursuit of it.

Look at our world today. Our youth have accepted lifestyles and bizarre issues that are an abomination to the Lord. Our adult population is spreading misinformation. Gossip is the tool of choice. Words are often not confirmed. "Be careful with your words, once they are said, they can only be forgiven, not forgotten" (anon). Once words are spoken into existence, they can never be retracted.

The Bible teaches that, *"Everyone should be quick to listen, slow to speak and slow to become angry"* (James 1:19). The world would be so much better if we only said words that were true, kind, and necessary.

It sometimes seems that people no longer have filters. Instead, we tell everyone what we think. Reputations can be destroyed in a second via today's internet and social media outlets.

> *"Finally, brothers and sisters, whatever is true, whatever is honorable, whatever is right, whatever is pure, whatever is lovely, whatever is commendable, if there is any excellence and if anything be worthy of praise, think on these things"* (Philippians 4:8 NASB).

While the peace of God guards our hearts and minds in Christ Jesus (Philippians 4:7), we are directed by God to focus our thoughts on things that are pleasing to God.

We all recently witnessed rioters looting and burning businesses on the streets of our cities. These mobs are said to communicate via the internet and assemble not to discuss issues but to destroy and steal.

These are truly feet that are swift in running to evil. People who love and fear the Lord do not behave in such a way.

King Solomon tells us that people's hearts are filled with schemes to do wrong when the sentence for a crime is not quickly carried out (Ecclesiastes 8:11). Man works to cover his tracks and justify his actions but only deceives himself by thinking he has gotten away with the sinful actions.

*"Does he who fashioned the ear not hear? Does he who formed the eye not see? Does he who disciplines nations not punish?"* (Psalm 94:9-10a).

A major influence in our lives is the people we spend time with. Who are our friends? What kind of people frequent the places we go to?

God's Word cautions us regarding those we "hang out with" saying, *"...my son, do not go along with them, do not set foot on their paths; for their feet rush into evil, they are swift to shed blood"* (Proverbs 1:15-16).

We may think we are influencing our friends, but most of us tend to go along with the crowd. Peer pressure is real and effective even after we become adults. I once heard of a Christian counselor advising a young woman concerning the company she was keeping. She was dating a non-Christian young man and hoped that she was influencing him for the better. He asked her, "If you throw a white glove in a mud puddle, does the glove become muddy or does the puddle becoming 'glovey'?" Sadly, she ignored his advice and suffered greatly.

How much better will our lives be if we heed the advice of Solomon ..."*Watch the path of your feet and all your ways will be established. Do not turn to the right nor to the left, turn your foot from evil*" (Proverbs 4:26-27 NASB).

- **A false witness who lies.** We have already touched on God's view of lying. He regards it as an abomination, as is *"one who sows discord among brethren"* (Proverbs 6:19).

Pat Robertson, in an article titled *"What Does It Mean to Bear False Witness,"* stated, "Starting lies about someone or spreading them is bearing false witness, a terrible offense in the sight of God."[16] Slander is one form of bearing false witness.

Who has never told a lie? Humans are imperfect, but, with the power of the Holy Spirit, we are commanded to refrain from lying.

> *"Therefore, putting away lying, Let each one of you speak truth with his neighbor"* **(Ephesians 4:25)**.

There are no caveats or exceptions. We tend to think some lying is acceptable. Even what we term as a "little white lie" is sin in God's eyes. Prosocial lies or lies of compassion seem to us to be the right thing to do under the circumstances.

Imagine you're at a friend's house and you're served a slice of apple pie. How do you respond when asked how you like it when you can barely eat it? Wanting to spare the baker's feelings, do you tell a little lie or the truth? Though it may be sometimes difficult to choose between honesty or compassion, the truth is always the best policy.

Ultimately, honesty creates stronger and more trusting relationships. Ask the Holy Spirit to guide you with your words, always speaking the truth in love, as we are admonished to do in Ephesians 4:15. Bear in mind that each lie you tell or each curse word you utter glorifies Satan and not the Lord. The more sinful a generation becomes, the less truth the people will tolerate.

The Apostle Paul warns us in Ephesians 4:29 to *"not let any unwholesome [filthy] talk come out of your mouths, but only what is helpful to building others up according to their needs, that it may benefit those who listen."* Paul reiterates in Ephesians 5:4, *"Nor*

---

[16] https://www1.cbn.com/questions/bear-false-witness

*should there be obscenity, foolish talk or coarse joking, which are out of place, but rather thanksgiving."*

Telling off-color jokes may entertain our friends or co-workers, but they are not funny to the Lord. Everyone wants to fit in or be popular. If we are popular, we are liked or admired by a lot of people or by a particular group. We may be popular or fit in because we are smart, a good athlete, have a good sense of humor, or any number of other reasons.

However, we are not called by God for any of these things. He had called us first to be His people and secondly to be a "Talmidim"—a disciple. We cannot win others to Christ by acting like the world.

*"The tongue has the power of life and death, and those who love it will eat its fruit"* (Proverbs 18:21).

Our words can bring folks closer to Jesus and the eternal life He brings. Our words can also lead people away from salvation to suffer eternity in hell (death).

- **One who sows discord among brethren.** Proverbs 6:14 tells us, *"Who plots evil with deceit in his heart, he always stirs up conflict"* (Proverbs 6:14). The intent of deception is to sow strife and disunity among brothers.

When we love wickedness and our own self-interests, rather than loving and being grateful to God, we create conflict with other people, including our families. Discord creates disharmony, while developing and nurturing godly relationships is an important part of maturing in the Lord.

# CHAPTER NINE

# DISCOVERING THE JOY OF OBEDIENCE

*"So if you faithfully obey the commands I am giving you today—to love the LORD your God and to serve him with all your heart and with all your soul—then I will send rain on your land in its season, both autumn and spring rains, so that you may gather in your grain, new wine and olive oil. I will provide grass in the fields for your cattle, and you will eat and be satisfied." (Deuteronomy 11:13-15)*

Obedience is critical to the joyful Christian life. The Lord's greatest blessings are bestowed on those who walk in His paths and abide in His Word. God often rewards the entire family of those who are obedient.

Hampered by our sin nature, we war against our flesh, the world, and our enemy Satan. The satanic realm takes full advantage of our weaknesses. Even the Apostle Paul struggled as we do. *"Now if I do what I do not want to do, it is no longer I who do it, but it is sin living in me that does it"* (Romans 7:20).

Over time, repetitive sin redefines our thinking to such an extent that we can lose our sensitivity to the voice of the Holy Spirit and grow callused consciences. When you first rake fallen leaves, your hands will hurt and blister. If you continue, calluses will eventually form, and pain will no longer be a factor. In much the same way, continuing in sin will at some point become normal, and the bitterness of sin no longer matters to us. As Christians, we now—through the Holy Spirit and the mighty name of Jesus—can resist temptation and refuse to continue in sin.

God will never allow us to be tempted more than we can bear.

> *"No temptation has overtaken you except what is common to mankind. And God is faithful; he will not let you be tempted beyond what you can bear. But when you are tempted, he will also provide a way out so that you can endure it"* (1 Corinthians 10:13).

How does the devil know our weaknesses? While he is not omniscient (he can't read our minds), he is wily and devious. He only needs to monitor our actions. If you watch dirty movies, he will tempt you with pornography. If you enjoy drinking socially, he will try to make you dependent on alcohol. If you do not take the sanctity of marriage seriously, he will be sure to give you opportunities to violate your vows.

Several years ago, Charlie Sheen starred in the television comedy, *Two and a Half Men*. His character was a hedonistic jingle writer who drank all day and was highly promiscuous. With this and other highly popular programs glorifying sex, alcohol, drugs, and other sins, it's no wonder young people conclude that sin is condoned and accepted by society.

It's easy to become addicted to sin. Habitual sin becomes a stronghold that only the Lord can break.

One of the important truths I hope you will learn from our time together in this book is that God never makes mistakes.

We are born male or female by His design and plan and for His purposes. The Lord wrote our stories before we were created. Paul writes in Romans 8:28, *"And we know that in all things God works for the good of those who love him, who have been called according to his purpose."*

If everything is pre-determined, what good is man's free will? Since God lives in eternity, He sees us from before our births, through every day of our lives, and He also sees us in death. He knows our desires, our faults, our strengths, and our weaknesses. While we make choices daily that determine the direction our lives take, the Lord knew what those choices would be before the beginning of time. Our choices are indeed our choices. We own them for good or for bad.

While our sin natures will be a part of us until we reach heaven, we who are born again have received the gift of the Holy Spirit who enables us to resist the schemes of the devil by submitting our lives to God and walking in His ways. We are helpless and weak without the Holy Spirit. But with His help, we can be always obedient in all ways!

## LET GOD BE YOUR GUIDE

Our very existence is dependent upon God, but we often fail to ask for His guidance before we undertake a course of action. On the other hand, we always turn to Him when things don't go as planned. We, like Adam, were created to depend on God.

We often mistakenly link dependence to weakness. Is it weak to think that God causes the sun to rise every morning or to depend on Him for our next breath or our health?

Jesus said, *"I am the vine, you are the branches. He who abides in Me, and I in him, bears much fruit; for without Me you can do nothing"* (John 15:5 NKJV). Without Jesus we can do nothing. Nothing.

We must choose to abide. Pastor James Montgomery Boice is quoted as saying, "When our Lord says: *Abide in me* He is talking about the will, about the choices, the decisions we make. We must decide to do things which expose ourselves to Him and keep ourselves in contact with Him. This is what it means to abide in Him."[17] Keep in mind this concept of abiding also means He is abiding in us. This keeps our lives connected, His life to ours and vice versa.

Depending on God is built into our DNA. It is not a weakness but simply identifies God's reality in this world. None of us is in control, as much as we'd like to think we are. We may think we control our households or those who are in our employ. (Though few of us would say we can control our spouses!) In truth, only God controls.

Another tool of the devil is to convince us to blame our parents for everything. While it is true that parents are highly influential and can harm their children through abuse and bad parenting, it is important to remember that, with the help of the Holy Spirit, we can shake ourselves free of our pasts and go on in freedom.

If we continue to lay the blame on our parents and elsewhere and do nothing to overcome our pasts, we will carry unnecessary baggage with us our entire lives. We cannot change the past. While no parent is perfect, most do the best they can with what they have. If you feel permanently marked by parental abuse, harboring anger and resentment can kill you.

---

[17] https://enduringword.com/bible-commentary/john-15/

*"Make every effort to live in peace with everyone and to be holy; without holiness no one will see the Lord. See to it that no one falls short of the grace of God and that no bitter root grows up to cause trouble and defile many"* (Hebrews 12:14-15).

Bitterness is toxic. It's a cancer. In 2011, Concordia University reported that constant bitterness can make a person sick.[18] Bitterness affects metabolism, immune response, and organ function and can lead to physical disease.

*"Let all bitterness and wrath and anger and clamor and slander be put away from you, along with all malice. Be kind to one another, tender hearted, forgiving each other, just as God in Christ also has forgiven you"* (Ephesians 4: 31-32 NASB).

Life is short. We may continue to "wallow in the mire," or decide to live life differently and abundantly through the sacrifice Jesus made for us all.

## DO YOU HAVE SPIRITUAL FATIGUE?

My intent in writing this book is to reach out and suggest a cure for spiritual fatigue. So many today are indifferent to spiritual issues. But I am convinced we are walking in the last days, and we must never lose hope. Christ is bigger than the fake news, the problems in the Middle East, the pandemics, the riots. He can handle it all.

---

[18] https://www.concordia.ca/cunews/main/releases/2011/08/09/can-blaming-others-make-people-sick.html

We must get this country back on track. Sadly, most are more concerned about sports and entertainment than about what happens to our souls at death.

Once the Lord takes His hand off our country, it will be over. Those who suggest we abandon Israel must be ignored. World events indicate we are rapidly moving toward a one-world government.

As a young man growing up in the fifties and sixties, I never could have predicted the state of the world today. It would have been ridiculous to suggest that the Catholic pope would align himself with the Muslims.

This historic interfaith covenant, signed in 2019 in Abu Dhabi, was kept under wraps and has recently been leaked to the press. Pope Francis and Ahmed al-Tayeb spearheaded the covenant and the concerted effort to ensure all of the religions of the world were represented at this gathering.

Our country's downward spiral will not be solved by covenants that God did not orchestrate. As a nation, we must remember that God is central to our escape from the lies of the last few years. The United States is no longer a superpower because of her moral decay.

Please pray for our country. And pray, also, for the peace of Jerusalem, and continue to support Israel at all times.

# CHAPTER TEN

# FILL THE EARTH

> "So God created mankind in his own image, in the image of God he created them; male and female he created them. God blessed them and said to them, 'Be fruitful and increase in number; fill the earth and subdue it. Rule over the fish in the sea and the birds in the sky and over every living creature that moves on the ground.'" (Genesis 1:27-2)

It has always been God's intention that man should *"fill the earth and subdue it,"* which is what He said to the first human beings shortly after they were created.

But, for some reason, human beings have always tended to cluster in one place. Yes, there have been pioneers and explorers among us—I think of people like Daniel Boone, Jedidiah Smith, and Lewis and Clark—who pushed the boundaries of the United States farther west. But there haven't been enough of them.

When I look around and see all the beautiful cultures God has created, it reminds me that He is a God of diversity. Just look at all the different kinds of beautiful flowers He created. Look at the birds. Everything from the little brown sparrow to the magnificent multi-colored peacock. The oceans are filled with amazing creatures, including some that provide their own light so they live in utter darkness on the sea floor. What amazing creativity our God displays.

And yet, mankind often fights against that diversity, striving for everything to be the same instead of different. We hear a lot of talk these days about how we are living in "one world," and we need to have one currency, one government, one way of life. But, as I said, this is not God's plan.

Genesis 11:1-8 tells us what happened when mankind attempted to build a tower to reach the heavens. This effort was an act to glorify themselves rather than God and demonstrate that they were in control of their own lives. It was also an attempt to keep human beings in one place.

Genesis 11:1-4 tells us,

> *"Now the whole world had one language and a common speech. As people moved eastward, they found a plain in Shinar and settled there. They said to each other, 'Come, let's make bricks and bake them thoroughly.' They used brick instead of stone, and tar for mortar. Then they said, 'Come, let us build ourselves a city, with a tower that reaches to the heavens, so that we may make a name for ourselves; otherwise we will be scattered over the face of the whole earth.'"*

In order to prevent the completion of this tower, God confused their language, making many languages where there had been only one. The people then had to separate into groups of those who spoke the same language. This confusion brought the tower construction to an abrupt end.

It also led to the fulfillment of God's plan for people to spread throughout the earth.

As we've seen, from the very beginning, it was God's plan to see the different cultures develop. But it was not His plan that these cultures would forget about Him or begin worshiping gods of their own making. When Jesus Christ died on the cross, He was paying the penalty for the sins of all mankind. Whoever comes to Jesus will be saved. Gender makes no difference. Neither does the color of skin. The language spoken. Or any other ethnic characteristic.

Thus, when the Apostle John is given a vision of the multitudes worshiping Jesus in heaven, he says, "

*"After this I looked, and there before me was a great multitude that no one could count, from every nation, tribe, people and language, standing before the throne and before the Lamb. They were wearing white robes and were holding palm branches in their hands"* (Revelation 7:9).

But it is important to understand that all of these people are worshiping before the throne because they have accepted Jesus as their Lord and Savior. For just as Jesus died for everyone, everyone who is redeemed must come to heaven through Him. There is no other way.

Sadly, there are almost as many beliefs about what happens after death as there are different cultures. Let's review a few of these beliefs.

## THE EGYPTIANS

The Egyptians paid homage to approximately two thousand gods. They believed in immortality, so corpses were embalmed, and the bodies of the pharaohs were also mummified to allow their souls to return to them.

As part of the burial ritual, priests pried open the mouth while pronouncing incantations and anointing the body to allow the dead person to speak, touch, smell, speak, and hear in the afterlife.

The Egyptians descended from Ham through Mizraim (Ham had four sons: Cush, Mizraim, Phut, and Canaan. See Genesis 10:6.)

## THE HITTITE EMPIRE

While the Hittites believed in an afterlife, there is little evidence that they prayed to gain heaven. They were descendants of Heth (son of Canaan, who was the son of Ham—Genesis 10:1-6).

The Hittite Empire reached its height around mid-1300 B.C. They believed that four gods sat on the throne in heaven. The Hittites were an eclectic group who did whatever they pleased, with little to no interest in God. They believed they would be able to hold on to their earthly possessions after death.

## THE CHINESE

Traditional burial practices indicate a belief in life after death and ancestral veneration. The Chinese gods number over a thousand, while about two hundred were actively worshipped.

The ancient Chinese prayed to their ancestors and to their multiple gods for help and protection. They believed they would continue to do the same things in the afterlife as they did in this life. Objects thought necessary to carry on their normal lives were buried with them.

Death brought peace and the souls of the dead remained to protect their descendants. The Chinese descended from the line of Ham.

## THE BABYLONIAN EMPIRE

Ancient Mesopotamians believed the afterlife was a land below our world called "Irkallu" or "Great Below."[19] Everyone went there after they died, regardless of their social status. While they primarily worshipped the god "Marduk," other gods were also venerated. They believed people lived in the afterlife as spirits or ghosts. Physical death meant little and did not disconnect them from life. No attempts were made to preserve the body, and the spirits were dreaded beings to the living. The Babylonians descended from Aram, the son of Shem.

## THE MUSLIMS

The Islamic faith believes that, on the last day, the dead will be resurrected to face judgement in accordance with their deeds. In order to be saved they must believe in the one God—Allah, and his prophet Muhammad.

## THE JEWS

The Jews believe in the ingathering of the exiled diaspora, the coming of the Jewish Messiah, and the revival of the dead. Their word for rapture is basically "end of days." Their end of days beliefs are as follows:

God will redeem the Jewish race and return them to the land of Israel. He will also restore the house of David and the Temple. The Messiah will lead the world (Messianic Age) in an age of justice and peace. He will then resurrect the dead,

---

[19] https://colors-newyork.com/what-is-mesopotamian-civilization-known-for/#Did_Mesopotamia_believe_in_afterlife

and all nations will recognize Him as the true God. Finally, He will create a New Heaven and a New Earth.

## WHAT ABOUT YOU?

What do you believe? Think seriously about what you will be thinking during the last minutes of your life.

Let's consider surgery. We may be frightened when we anticipate an operation, but we are usually convinced it's something that must be done to bring us back to good health. We desperately hope the surgeon, anesthesiologist, and surgical staff are skillful and focused. Anticipation, worry, and anxiety cause us to lose sleep and bring more stress. In the end, we have no options.

The best news is to wake up and hear the words that the surgery was a success, and a mountain is lifted from our shoulders. And that's just surgery.

Let's consider what we go through when facing death.

Christians believe that Christ paid the penalty for their sins. Jesus' atonement on the cross and His resurrection are part of God's plan to redeem mankind. Once Adam sinned, mankind was doomed because all men descended from Adam. While we face death, our only option is to trust what God did for us. God gave us a gift—grace—and all we need to do is accept His Gift. No works, no climbing the Vatican stairs on your knees, no masses, not even keeping the Ten Commandments. The Ten Commandments (Law) cannot save us. We all are saved by grace. *"For it is by grace you have been saved, through faith—and this is not from yourselves, it is the gift of God—"* (Ephesians 2:8). Works cannot save us (*"...not by works, so that no one can boast"* Ephesians 2:9).

In our last moments, our breathing most likely changes, becoming slower, noisier, and shallow--changes brought about by a reduction in blood flow. Facial muscles relax and begin to pale. Eyes and mouth droop. But the most important thing is not the physical death of the body but spiritual death. We were born going to hell. But God's plan to save us and take us to heaven is found in the finished work of Christ.

## IS THE RAPTURE IN OUR FUTURE?

Bible scholar, Dr. David Jeremiah, wrote a short article titled, *What Is the Difference Between the Rapture and the Second Coming?*

In this article he tells us that the two events are distinct—and have distinct purposes. He explains the difference saying, "At the Rapture, Jesus will return *for* His saints. At the Second Coming, He will return *with* His saints. At the Rapture, Jesus will not descend to earth. At the Second Coming, He will descend to the Mount of Olives as a prelude to His earthly reign.

"At the Rapture, Jesus will bring a blessing for His saints. At the Second Coming, He will bring judgment for those who have rejected Him.

"The Rapture could occur at any moment. The Second Coming will occur seven years later.

"When the Rapture occurs, Christ will take every deceased and every living Christian to heaven with Him. Paul describes this glorious event in 1 Thessalonians 4:16–17:

> *'For the Lord Himself will descend from heaven with a shout, with the voice of an archangel, and with the trumpet of God. And the dead in Christ will rise first. Then we who are alive and remain shall be caught up together with them in the clouds to meet the Lord in the air. And thus we shall always be with the Lord.'*

"The Rapture will protect God's saints from the Tribulation—the seven years of judgment that will be poured out on earth between the Rapture and the Second Coming. There are some who argue the Tribulation period will begin before the Rapture. However, the Bible says that *"there is therefore now no condemnation to those who are in Christ Jesus"* (Romans 8:1), which suggests the Church will not experience God's judgment during the Tribulation.

Seven years after the Rapture, Jesus will return to earth in the event known as the Second Coming. His return will be entirely different from His arrival in Bethlehem as a humble Child.

When Christ returns, He will appear as the exalted King of the universe, surrounded by His saints. The powers of evil will be quickly defeated at the Battle of Armageddon, and then Christ will establish His everlasting kingdom on earth."[20]

## WHAT WILL THE AFTERLIFE BE LIKE?

For the Christian, the afterlife includes a New Heaven and a New Earth. There is no pain or suffering and no purgatory. We will no longer have a sin nature, but we will still have free will.

What will we do in heaven? First, God will wipe all the tears from our eyes. As there is no sadness in heaven, I believe we will be unaware if any of our loved ones are not there.

Heaven is a holy place, a paradise we are incapable of even imagining, where God's will is done always.

People who think heaven will be boring will be greatly surprised. Our God, in His love and kindness, is never boring.

---

[20] https://www.davidjeremiah.org/age-of-signs/what-is-the-difference-between-the-rapture-and-the-second-coming

In this life, we have been happy, sad, fearful, angry. We have bad habits and so many things we dislike. In heaven we will never be in need of anything. We are loved by the Creator of the universe. God created everything for us to enjoy.

Heaven is our real home, and there we will experience absolute joy, as we share in God's presence and riches. We will see the Lord face to face. I believe we will live like Adam and Eve before the fall, walking and fellowshipping with the Lord daily. No sickness. No crying. No pain. Just the pleasures the Lord provided since the beginning of time.

*"You make known to me the path of life; you will fill me with joy in your presence, with eternal pleasures at your right hand"* (Psalm 16:11).

*"However, as it is written: 'What no eye has seen, what no ear has heard, and what no human mind has conceived'— the things God has prepared for those who love him—"* (1 Corinthians 2-9).

We will recognize and talk with Abraham, Moses, David, and all the Christians who have gone before us. There will be no competition. No pride, jealousy, or discrimination. We will once again speak one language. (I think we may speak Hebrew as there are no curse words in that language.) Nothing will thwart Christian fellowship. Nothing will hinder corporate praise and worship. We will all be united in loving God, thanking Him, and seeking His Glory alone.

I also believe we will get back that part of our brain we lost at the fall. Knowledge will be incredible and will enable us to understand more about God and His grace.

There will be work. We will all have God-given jobs. Not like we worked on earth, as there will be no pay other than the joy of doing whatever task God assigns. I believe this is so because work was originally part of God's plan in the Garden of Eden (see Genesis 2:15).

## A QUICK RECAP

So, let's take a moment to recap what we've said.

**Heaven is a real, not mythical, place with many dwelling places.**

> *"My Father's house has many rooms; if that were not so, would I have told you that I am going there to prepare a place for you? And if I go and prepare a place for you, I will come back and take you to be with me that you also may be where I am"* (John 14: 2-3).

**Heaven will be a city built for worship.**

> *"But you have come to Mount Zion, to the city of the living God, the heavenly Jerusalem. You have come to thousands upon thousands of angels in joyful assembly, to the church of the firstborn, whose names are written in heaven. You have come to God, the Judge of all, to the spirits of the righteous made perfect..."* (Hebrews *12:22-23*).

***It will be a place for all nations and peoples to worship Jesus.***

> *"After this I looked, and there before me was a great multitude that no one could count, from every nation, tribe, people and language, standing before the throne and before the Lamb. They were wearing white robes and were holding palm branches in their hands. And they cried out in a loud voice: 'Salvation belongs to our God, who sits on the throne, and to the Lamb'"* (Revelation 7:9-10).

***Heaven will be a place of peace, filled with joy and praise.***

> *"Therefore, they are before the throne of God and serve him day and night in his temple; and he who sits on the throne will shelter them with his presence. Never again will they hunger; never again will they thirst. The sun will not beat down on them, nor any scorching heat. For the Lamb at the center of the throne will be their shepherd; he will lead them to springs of living water. And God will wipe away every tear from their eyes" (Revelation 7:15-17).*

The entire city will be adorned with precious gemstones (see Revelation 21:9-11), and we will walk on streets paved with pure gold. All this, as we reunite with our loved ones, a perfect rest for our new, glorified bodies.

## HELL IS REAL

If this is heaven, what then is hell?

The Bible describes hell as outer darkness, a place of weeping and gnashing of teeth (see Matthew 8:12 and 13:42). Scripture is also clear that hell is a place of flames.

> *"So he called to him, 'Father Abraham, have pity on me and send Lazarus to dip the tip of his finger in water and cool my tongue, because I am in agony in this fire'"* (Luke 16:24).

Isaiah 33:14 also made clear the agonies of hell.

> *"The sinners in Zion are terrified; trembling grips the godless: 'Who of us can dwell with the consuming fire? Who of us can dwell with everlasting burning?'"*

In an article written by Terry Watkins called, *"The Truth About Hell,"*[21] the author states that there are 162 references to a place called hell, 70 of which were uttered by the Lord Himself. Hell is a place of fire, a place of darkness. Can you imagine anything worse than darkness so deep you cannot see your hand in front of your eyes? And then there is the fire that burns but does not consume, keeping its inhabitants in constant pain, constant torture.

Where is hell? The Bible is clear that it is inside the earth.

*"What does 'he ascended' mean except that he also descended to the lower, earthly regions?"* (Ephesians 4:9).

**The most important thing to remember on your death bed is to say, "Jesus save me."**
Understanding this book is easy if you believe in the Lord. If you do not believe or are on the fence, I urge you to consider your plan for gaining heaven. Consider all the other religions in this world and see if any measure up to your expectations. Your eternity hangs in the balance.

Jesus died for you. He died for me and for all mankind. Trusting in what God the Father did by placing all of man's sin on Christ as He hung on the cross is truly an act of love for man. Acknowledging and trusting the finished work of Christ on the cross is accepting, by faith, God's ultimate gift that lays waste to the ultimate plague of sin.

I wish I could say I am not afraid of death. Perhaps apprehensive is a better word. I do know that I will be in heaven someday, not because I'm a good person or did much for my fellow man, but because I truly trust in Jesus and the work He completed on the cross on my behalf. I am a sinner saved by the grace of God, and for that I will be eternally grateful to my Heavenly Father.

---

[21] https://www2.gvsu.edu/pontiusd/hell.html

www.ingramcontent.com/pod-product-compliance
Ingram Content Group UK Ltd.
Pitfield, Milton Keynes, MK11 3LW, UK
UKHW022222230426
12048UKWH00016BA/1005